BookLife GRAPHIC READERS

APOCALYPSE NAN

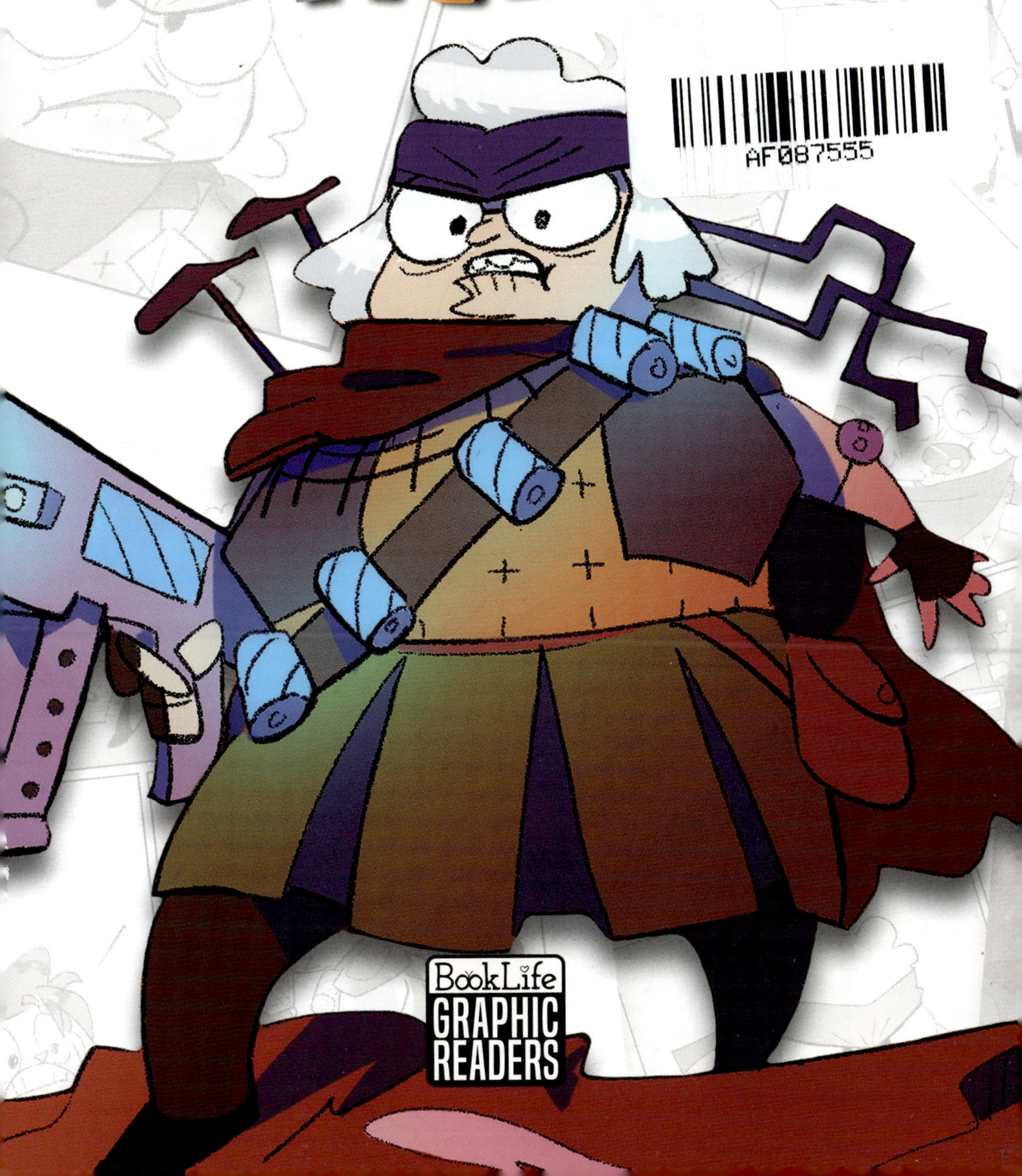

BookLife GRAPHIC READERS

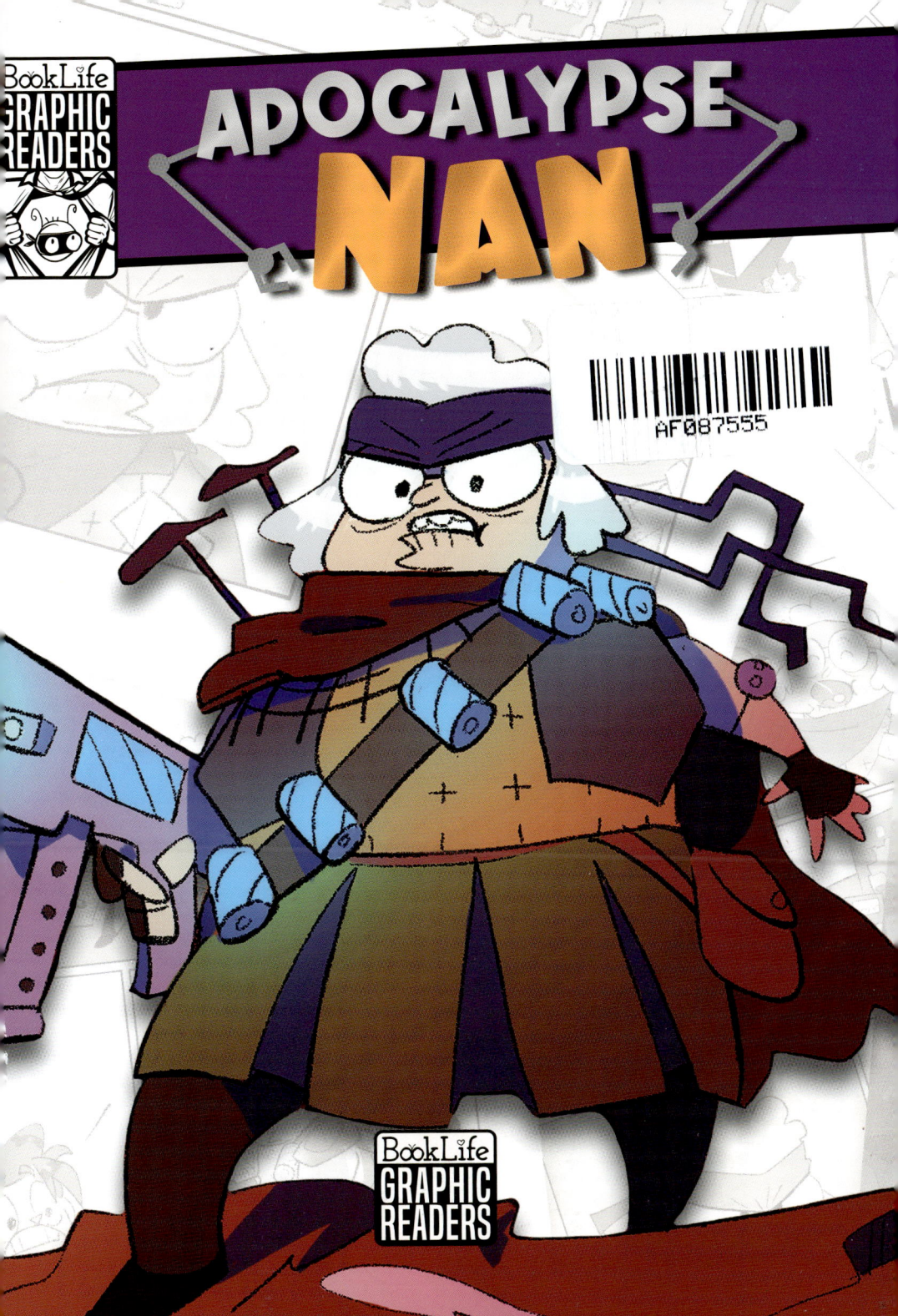

HOW TO READ A COMIC BOOK

Comic books are made up of pictures in boxes, called panels. Look at each of these panels from left to right, and top to bottom.

Read the speech bubbles, caption boxes and any sound effects from left to right, too. Together with the images, these will tell you the story.

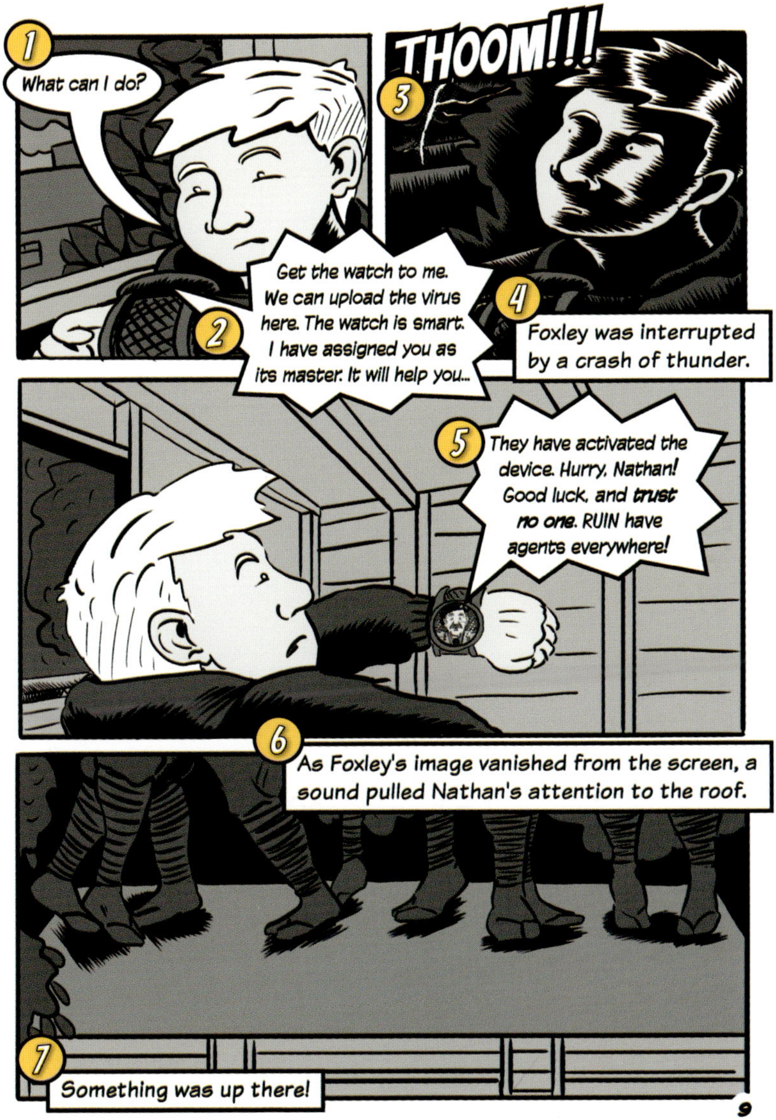
1
What can I do?
2
Get the watch to me. We can upload the virus here. The watch is smart. I have assigned you as its master. It will help you...
THOOM!!!
3
4
Foxley was interrupted by a crash of thunder.
5
They have activated the device. Hurry, Nathan! Good luck, and ***trust no one***. RUIN have agents everywhere!
6
As Foxley's image vanished from the screen, a sound pulled Nathan's attention to the roof.
7
Something was up there!

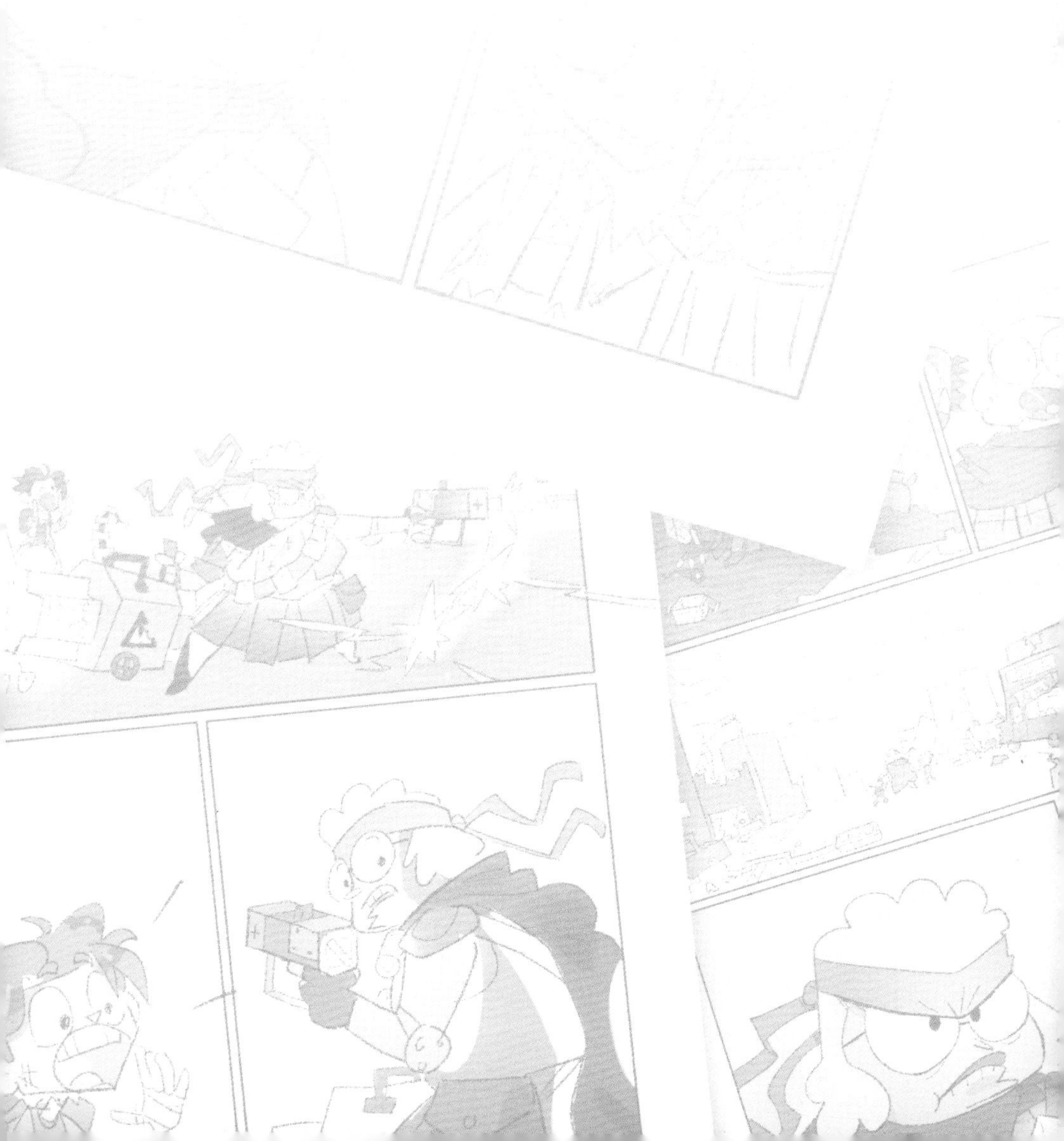

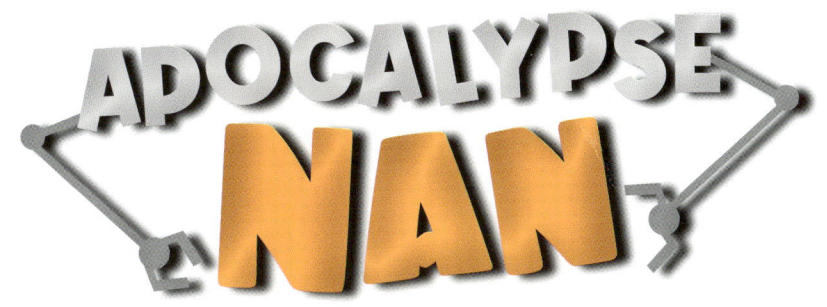

APOCALYPSE NAN

Written by
ROBIN TWIDDY

Illustrated by
ALEX WATTS

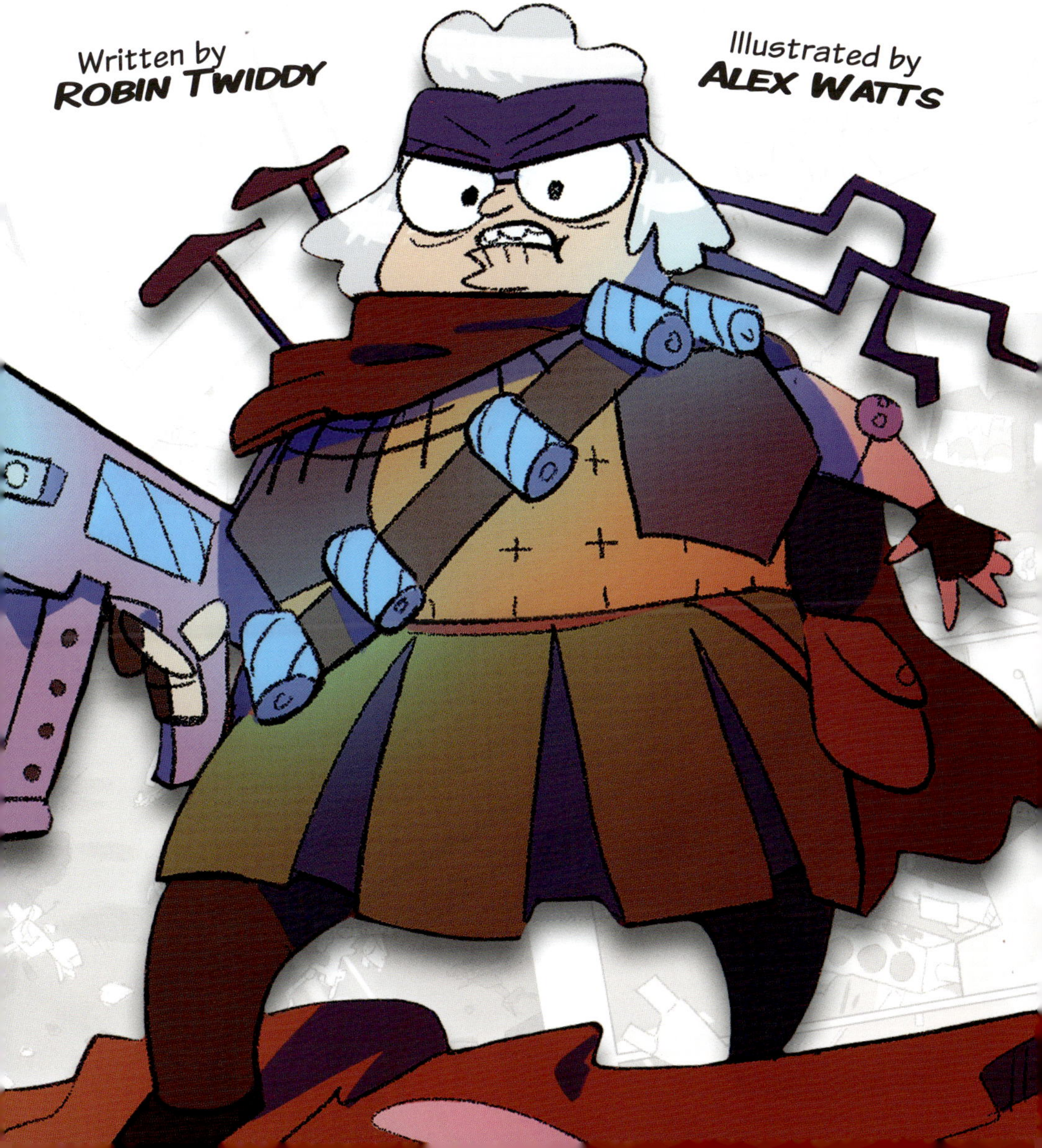

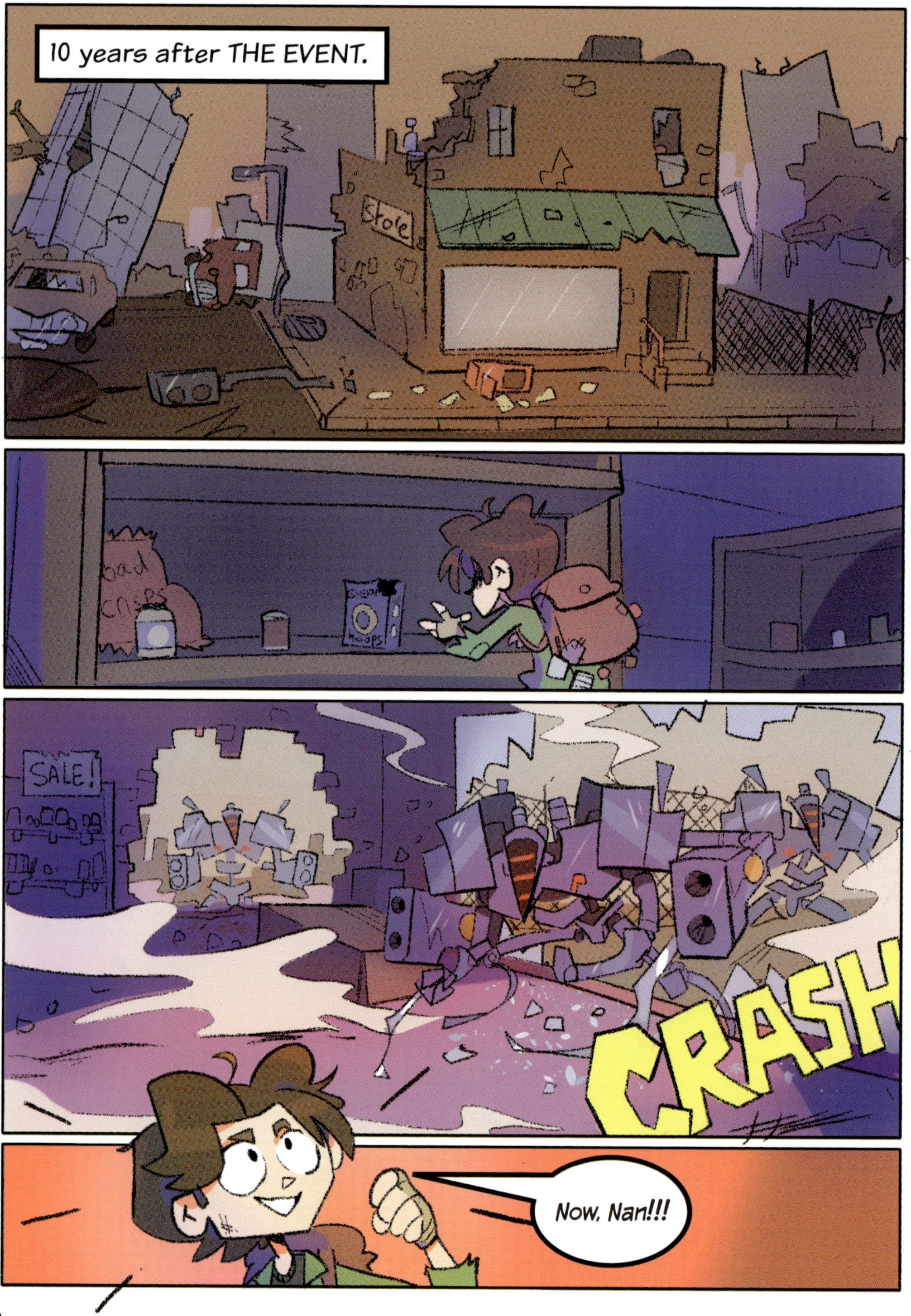
10 years after THE EVENT.
Store
bad crisps
Hoops
SALE!
CRASH
Now, Nan!!!

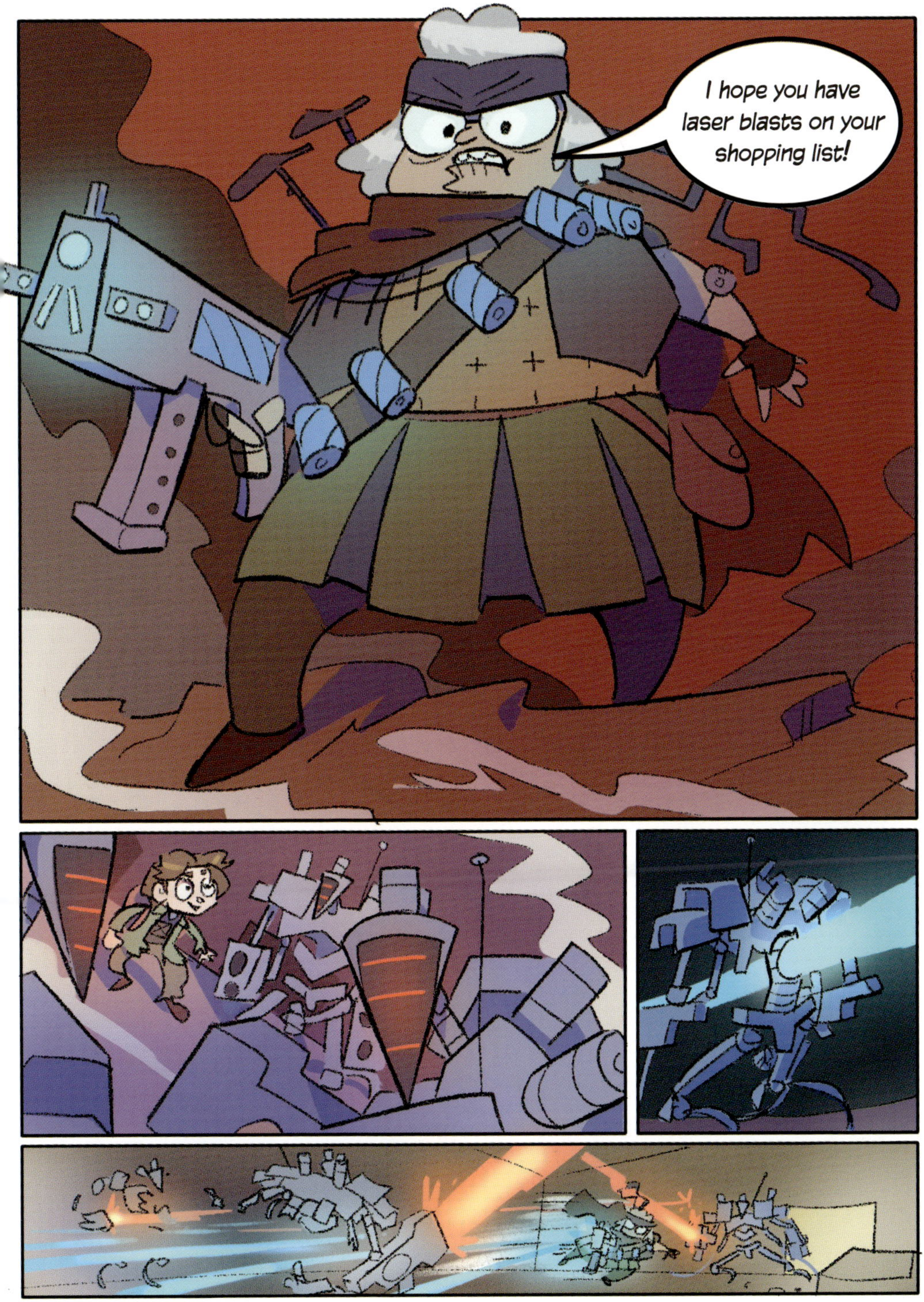
I hope you have laser blasts on your shopping list!

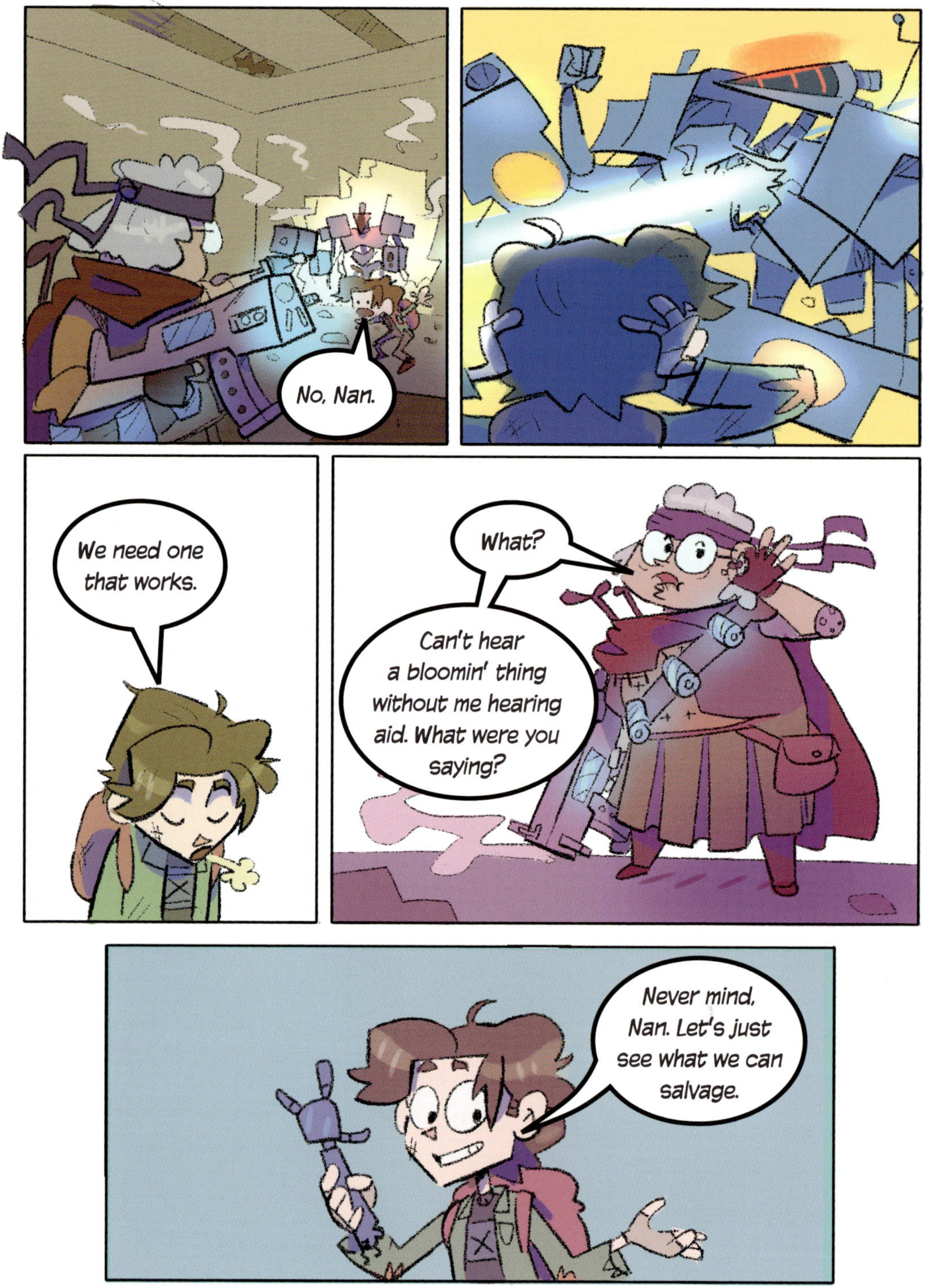
No, Nan.
We need one that works.
What?
Can't hear a bloomin' thing without me hearing aid. What were you saying?
Never mind, Nan. Let's just see what we can salvage.

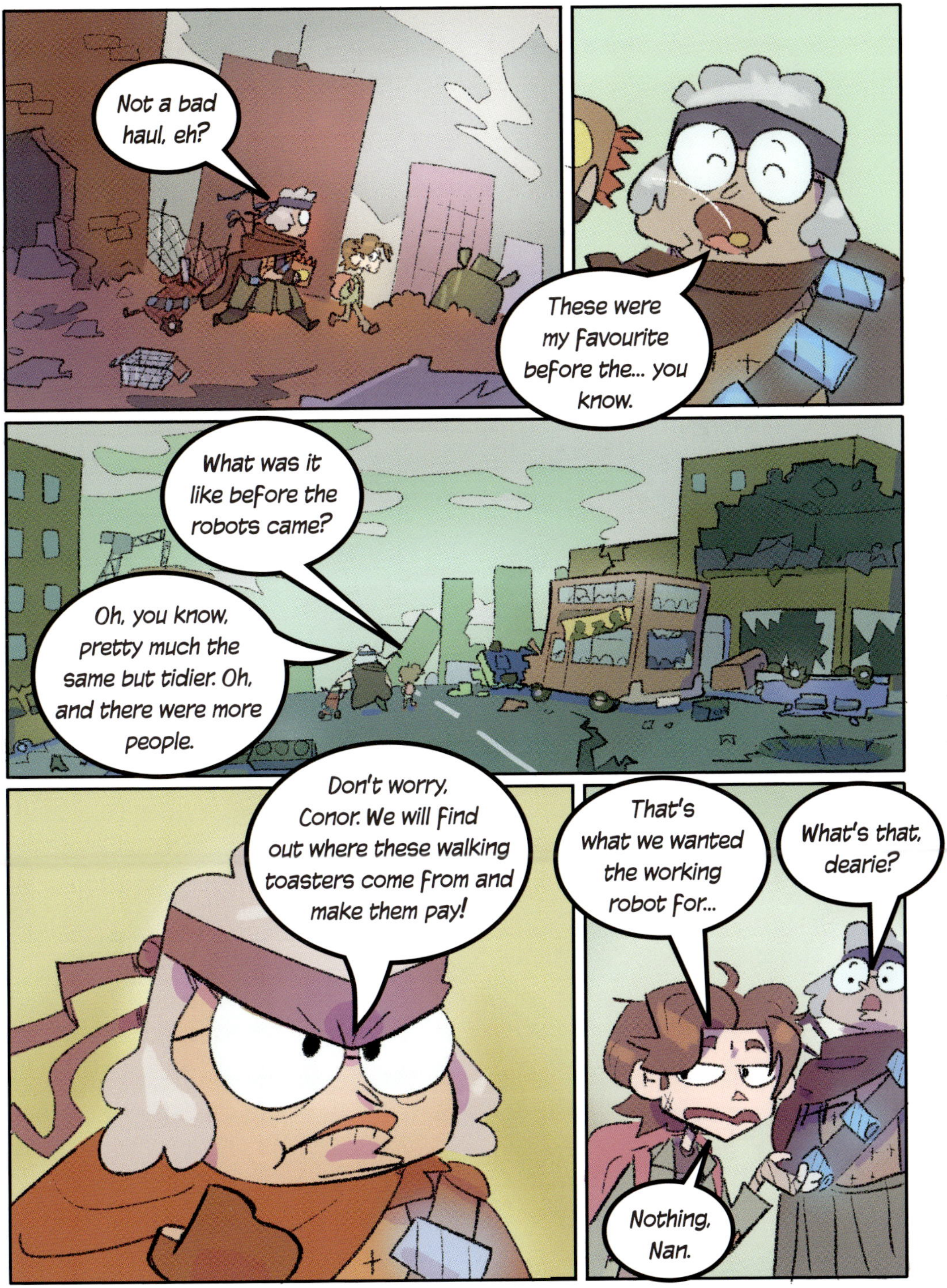
Not a bad haul, eh?
These were my favourite before the... you know.
What was it like before the robots came?
Oh, you know, pretty much the same but tidier. Oh, and there were more people.
Don't worry, Conor. We will find out where these walking toasters come from and make them pay!
That's what we wanted the working robot for...
What's that, dearie?
Nothing, Nan.

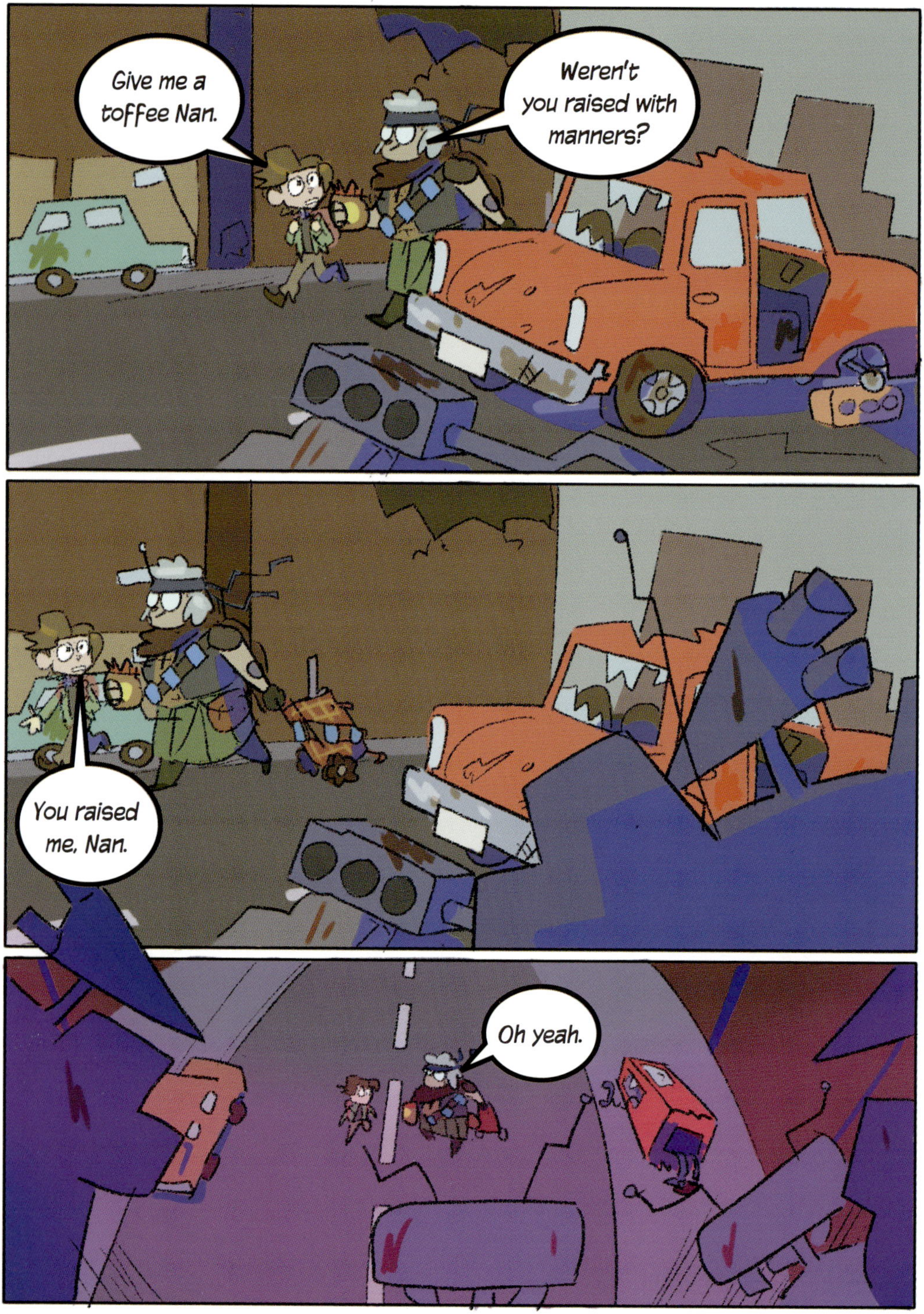
Give me a toffee Nan.
Weren't you raised with manners?
You raised me, Nan.
Oh yeah.

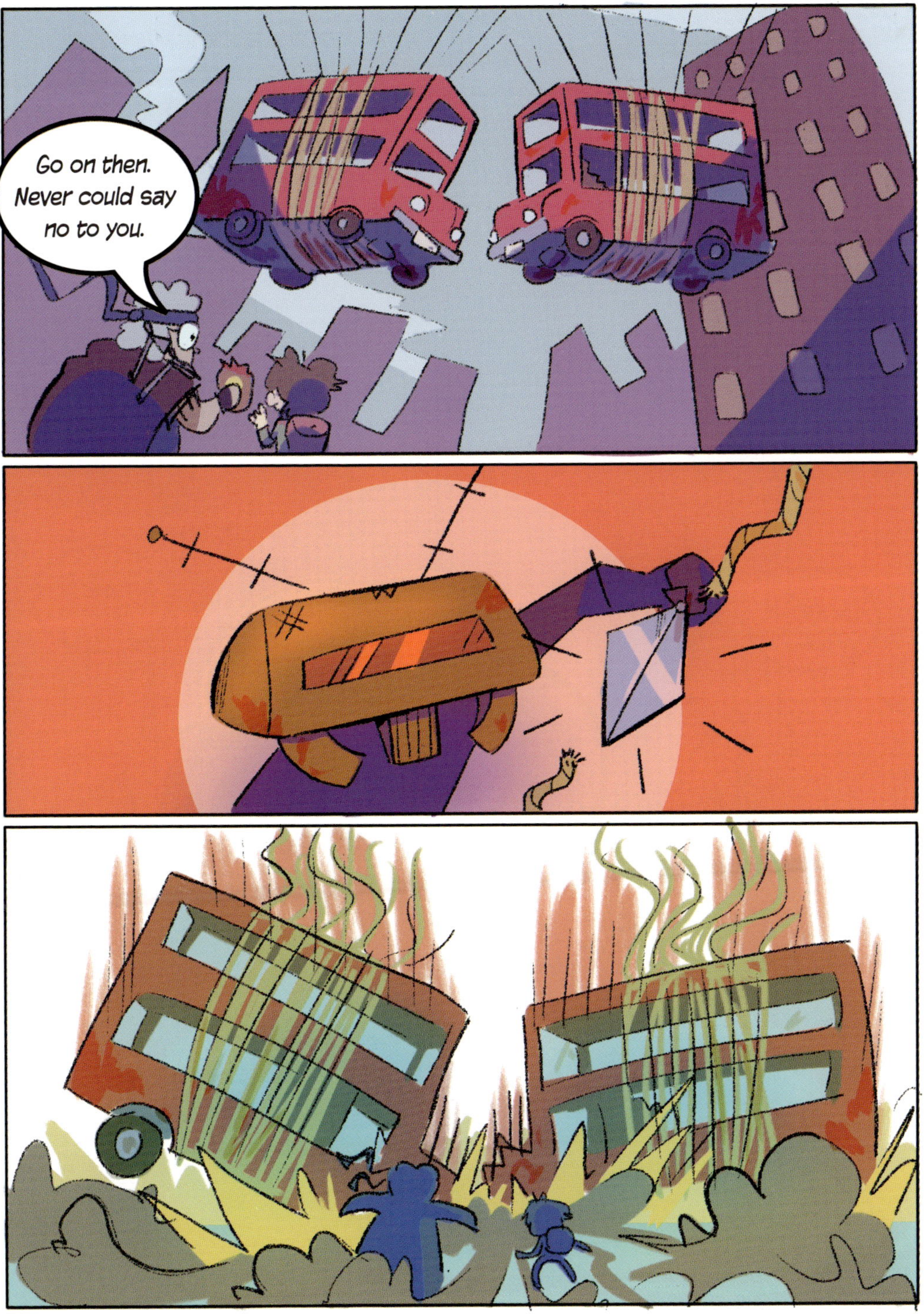
Go on then. Never could say no to you.

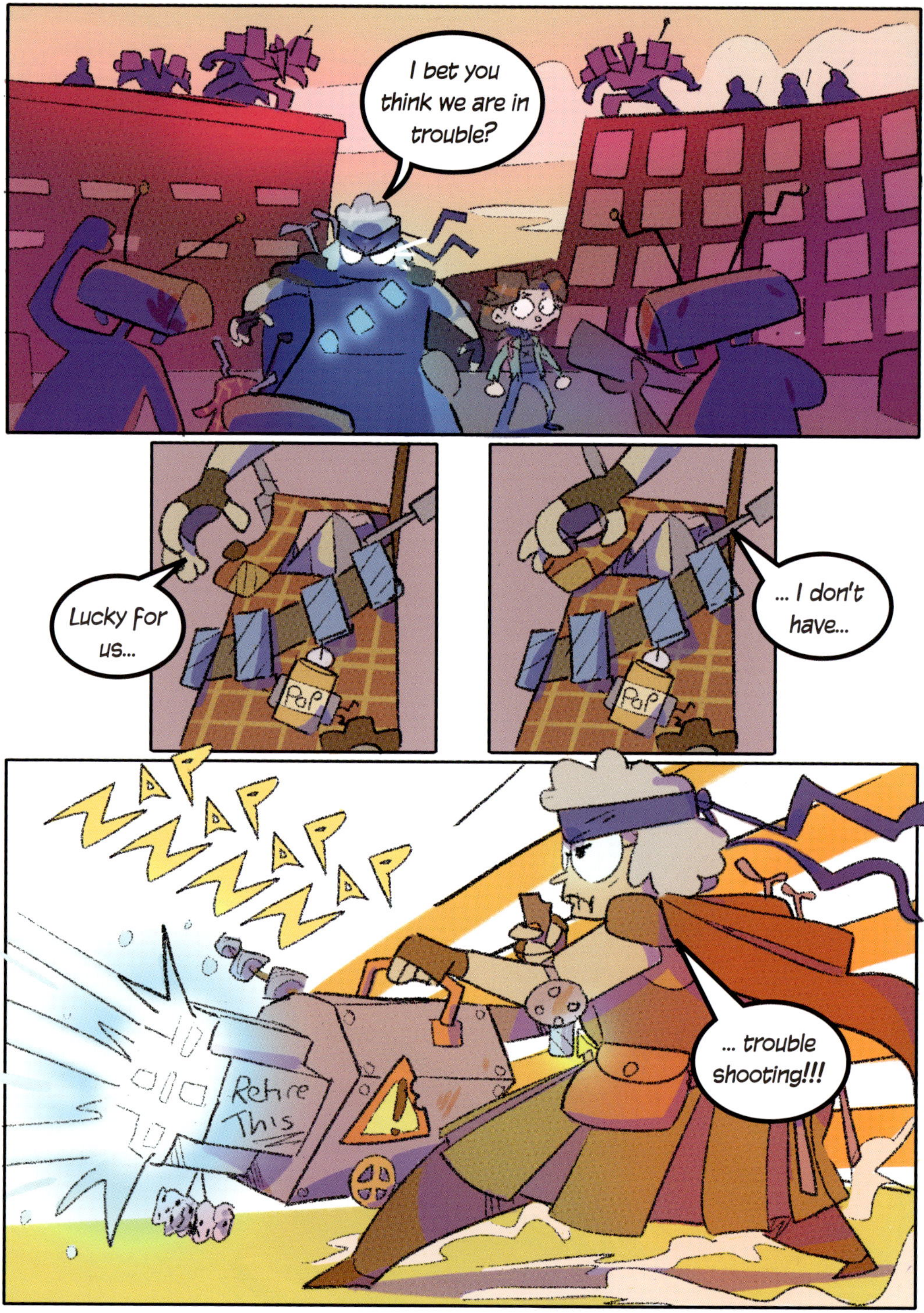
I bet you think we are in trouble?
Lucky for us...
... I don't have...
ZAP ZAP ZAP ZAP ZAP
Retire This
... trouble shooting!!!

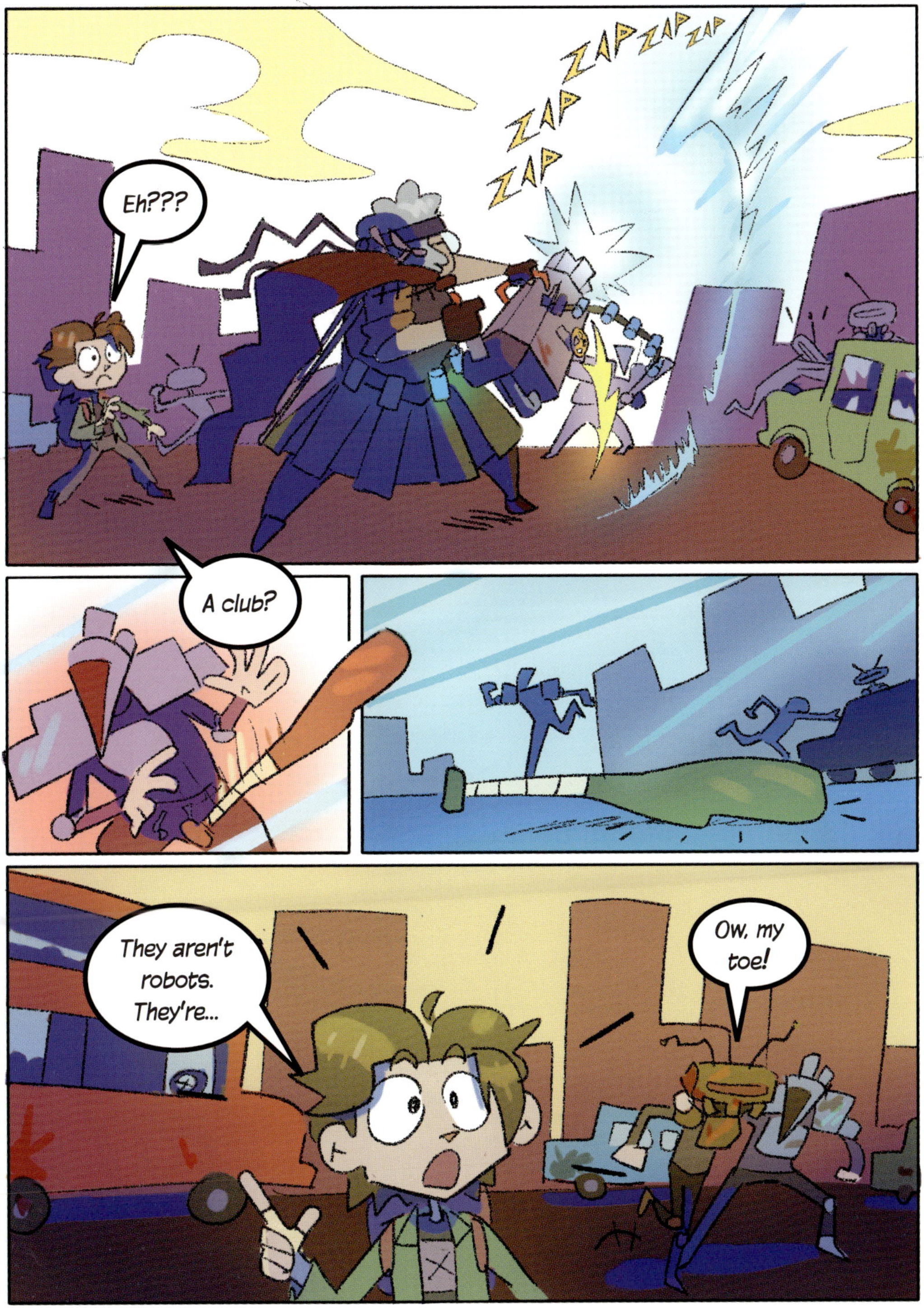
Eh???
ZAP ZAP ZAP ZAP ZAP
A club?
They aren't robots. They're...
Ow, my toe!

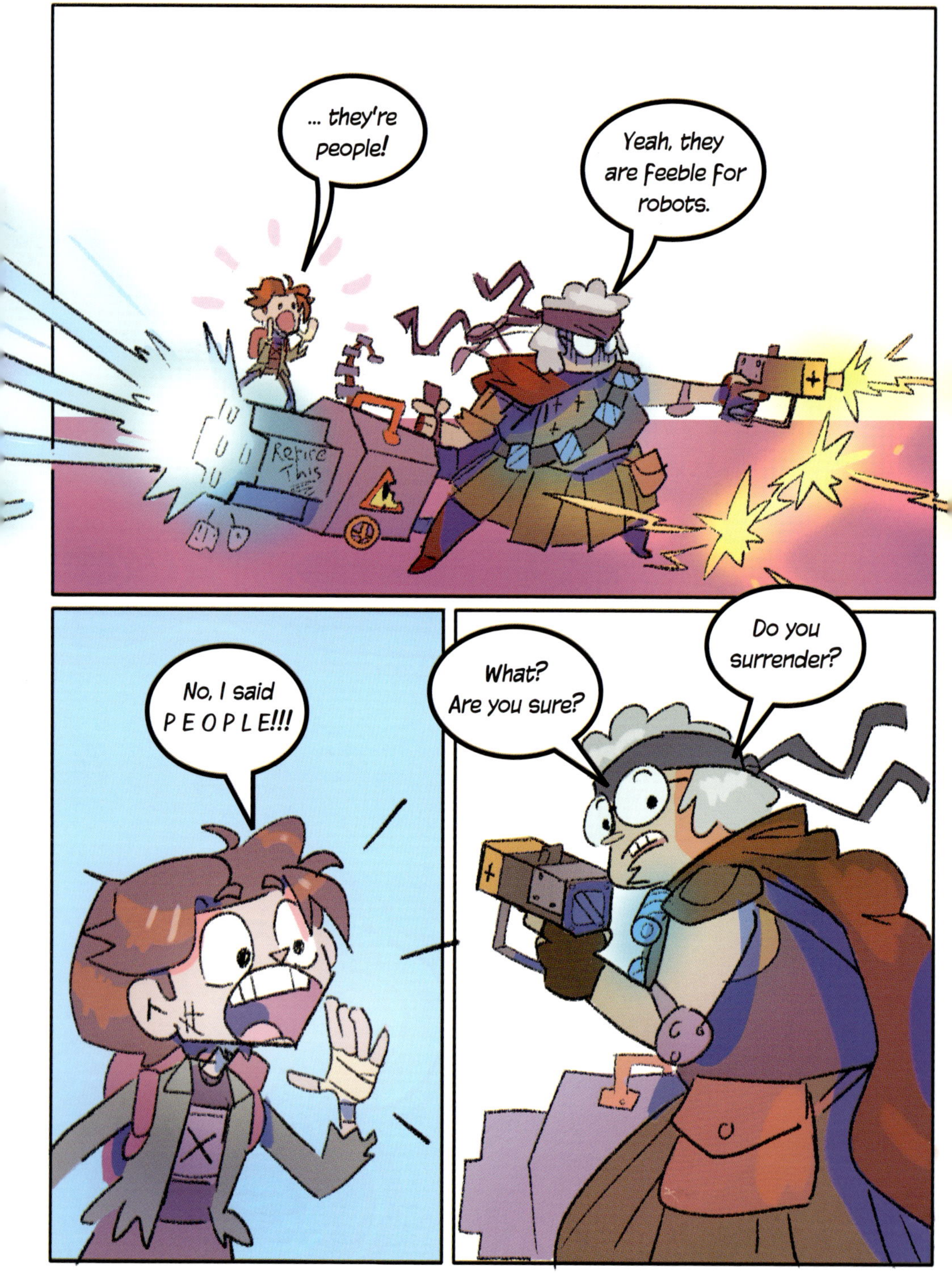

... they're people!
Yeah, they are feeble for robots.
Retire This
No, I said P E O P L E!!!
What? Are you sure?
Do you surrender?

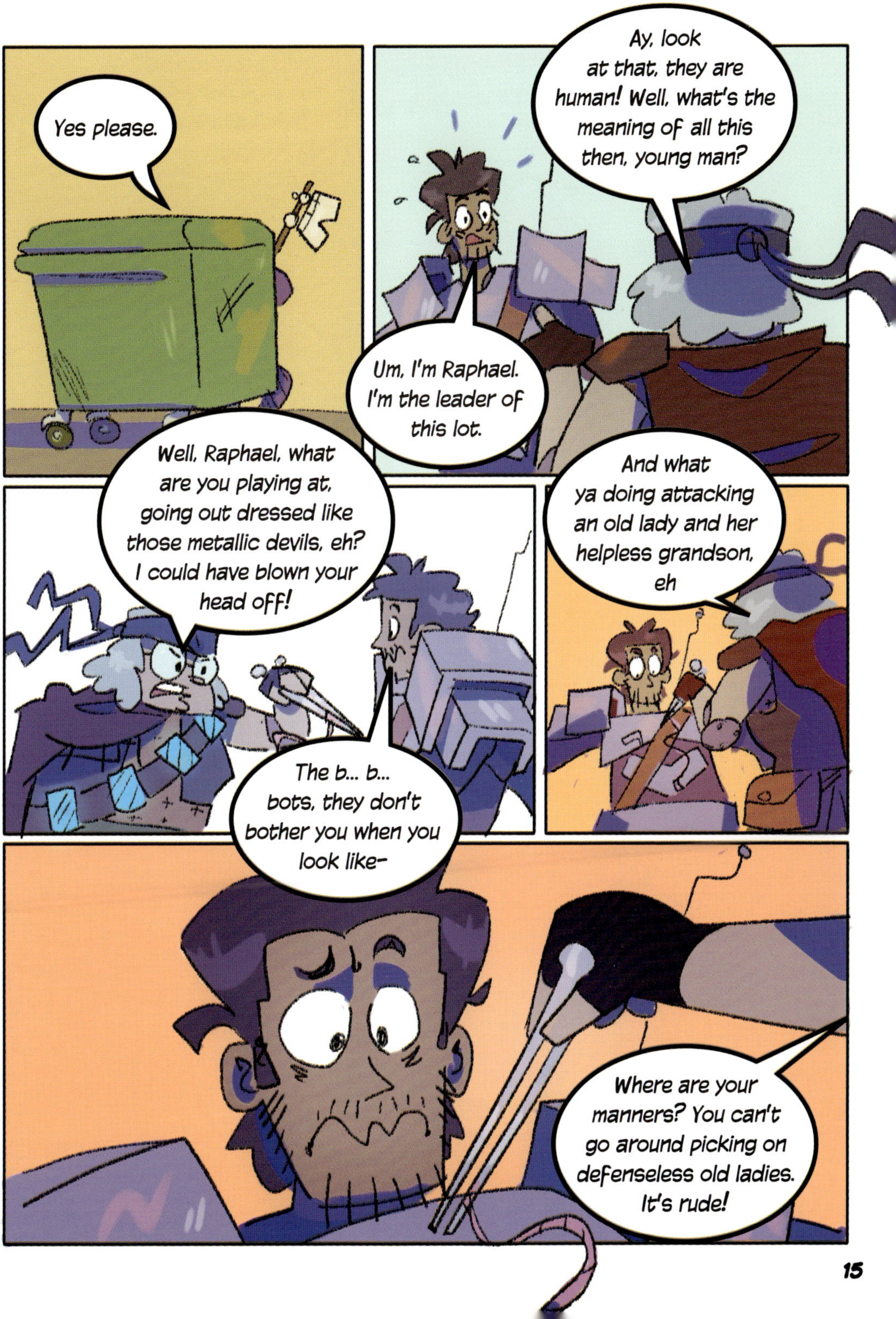
Yes please.
Ay, look at that, they are human! Well, what's the meaning of all this then, young man?
Um, I'm Raphael. I'm the leader of this lot.
Well, Raphael, what are you playing at, going out dressed like those metallic devils, eh? I could have blown your head off!
The b... b... bots, they don't bother you when you look like-
And what ya doing attacking an old lady and her helpless grandson, eh
Where are your manners? You can't go around picking on defenseless old ladies. It's rude!

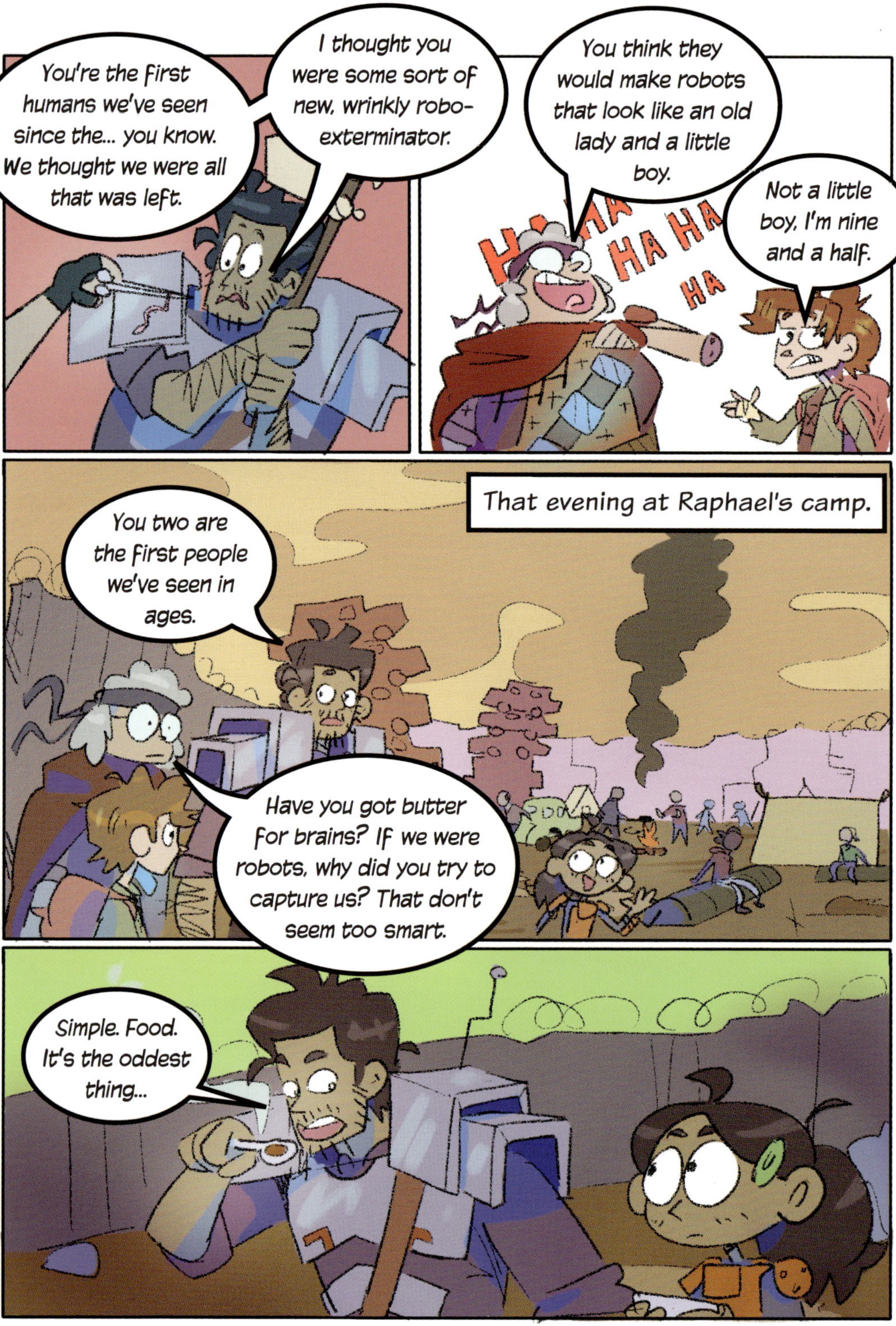

You're the first humans we've seen since the... you know. We thought we were all that was left.
I thought you were some sort of new, wrinkly robo-exterminator.
You think they would make robots that look like an old lady and a little boy.
HA HA HA HA
Not a little boy, I'm nine and a half.
That evening at Raphael's camp.
You two are the first people we've seen in ages.
Have you got butter for brains? If we were robots, why did you try to capture us? That don't seem too smart.
Simple. Food. It's the oddest thing...

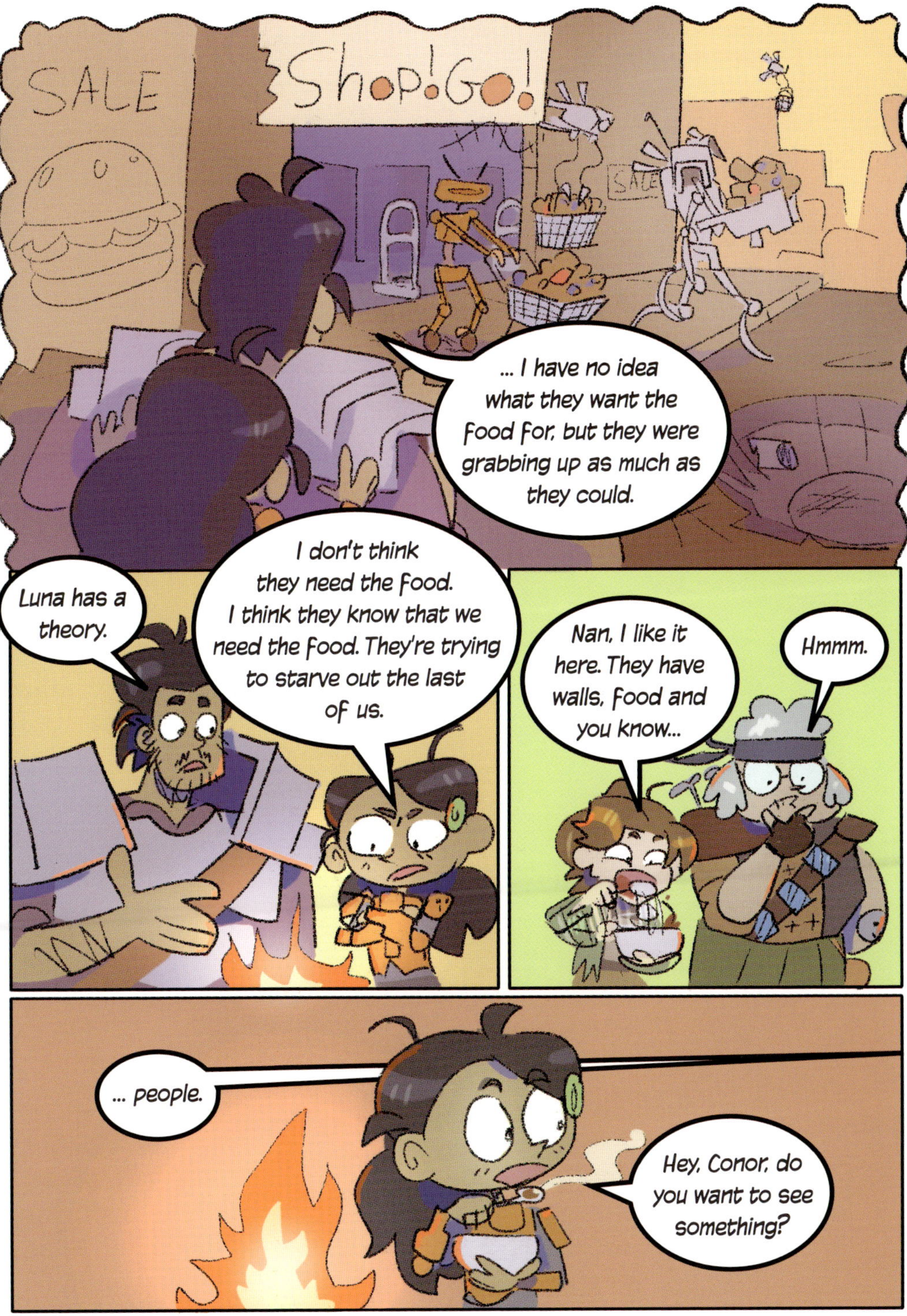
SALE
Shop!Go!
SALE
... I have no idea what they want the food for, but they were grabbing up as much as they could.
Luna has a theory.
I don't think they need the food. I think they know that we need the food. They're trying to starve out the last of us.
Nan, I like it here. They have walls, food and you know...
Hmmm.
... people.
Hey, Conor, do you want to see something?

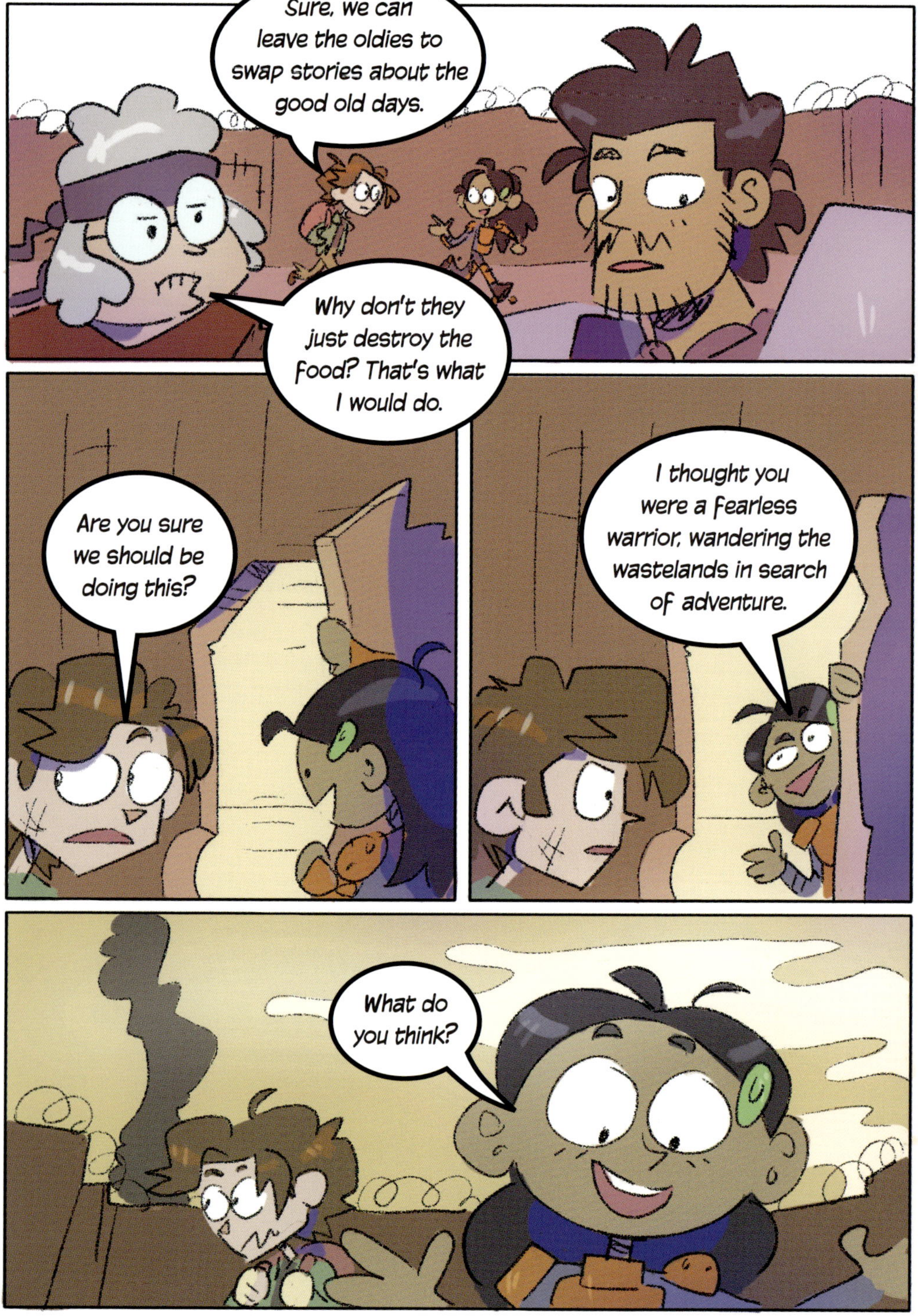
Sure, we can leave the oldies to swap stories about the good old days.
Why don't they just destroy the food? That's what I would do.
Are you sure we should be doing this?
I thought you were a fearless warrior, wandering the wastelands in search of adventure.
What do you think?

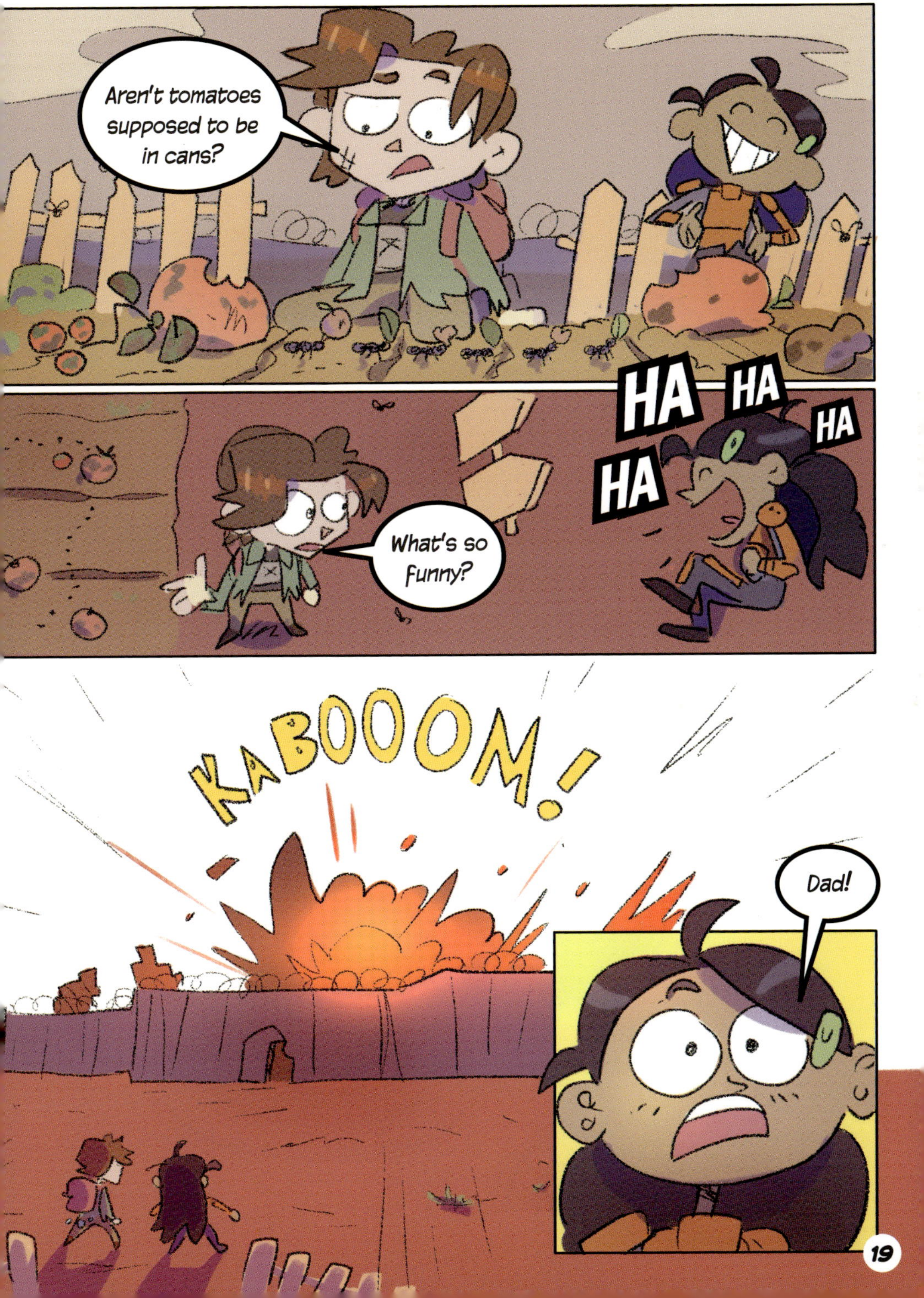
Aren't tomatoes supposed to be in cans?
HA HA HA HA
What's so funny?
KABOOOM!
Dad!

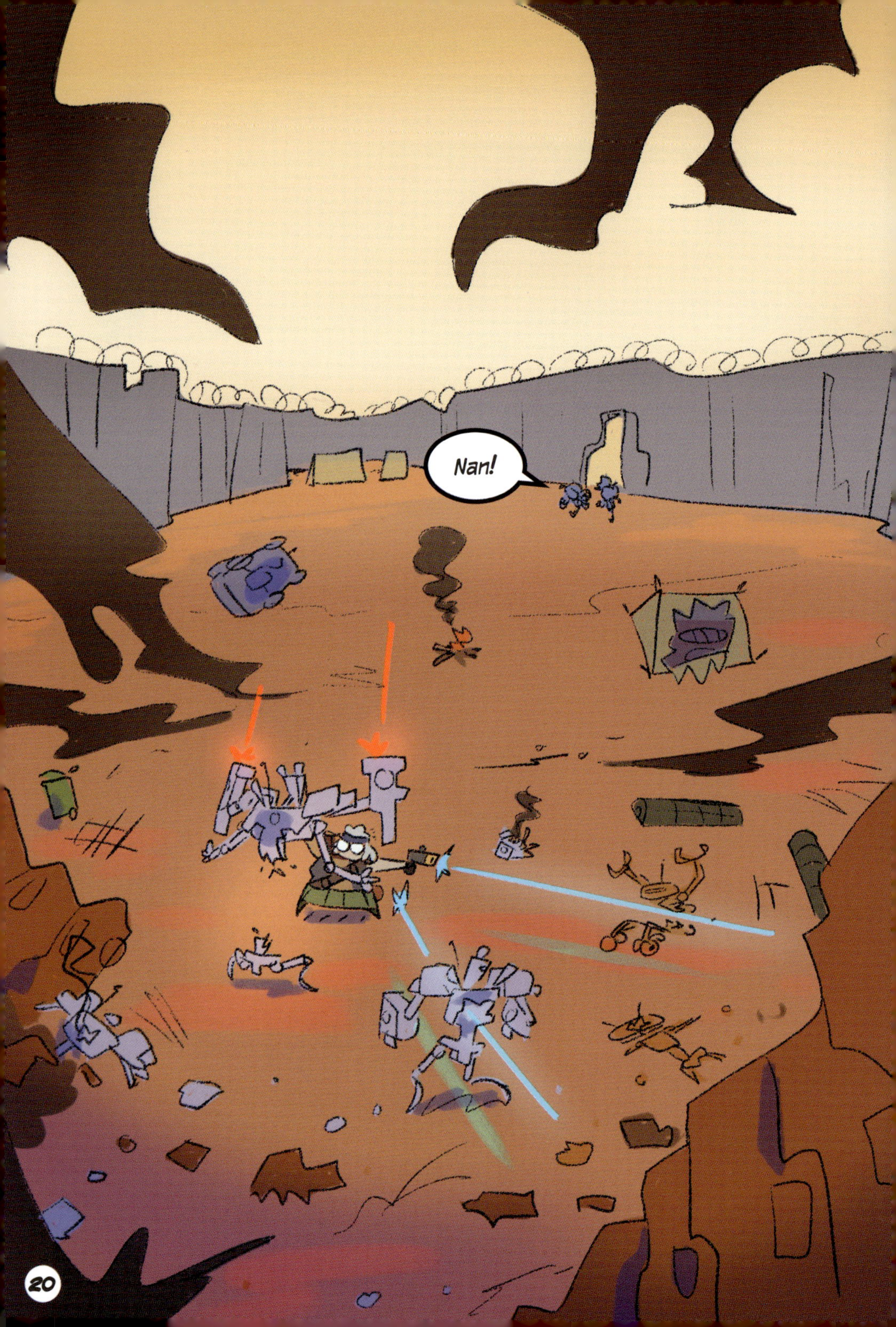
Nan!

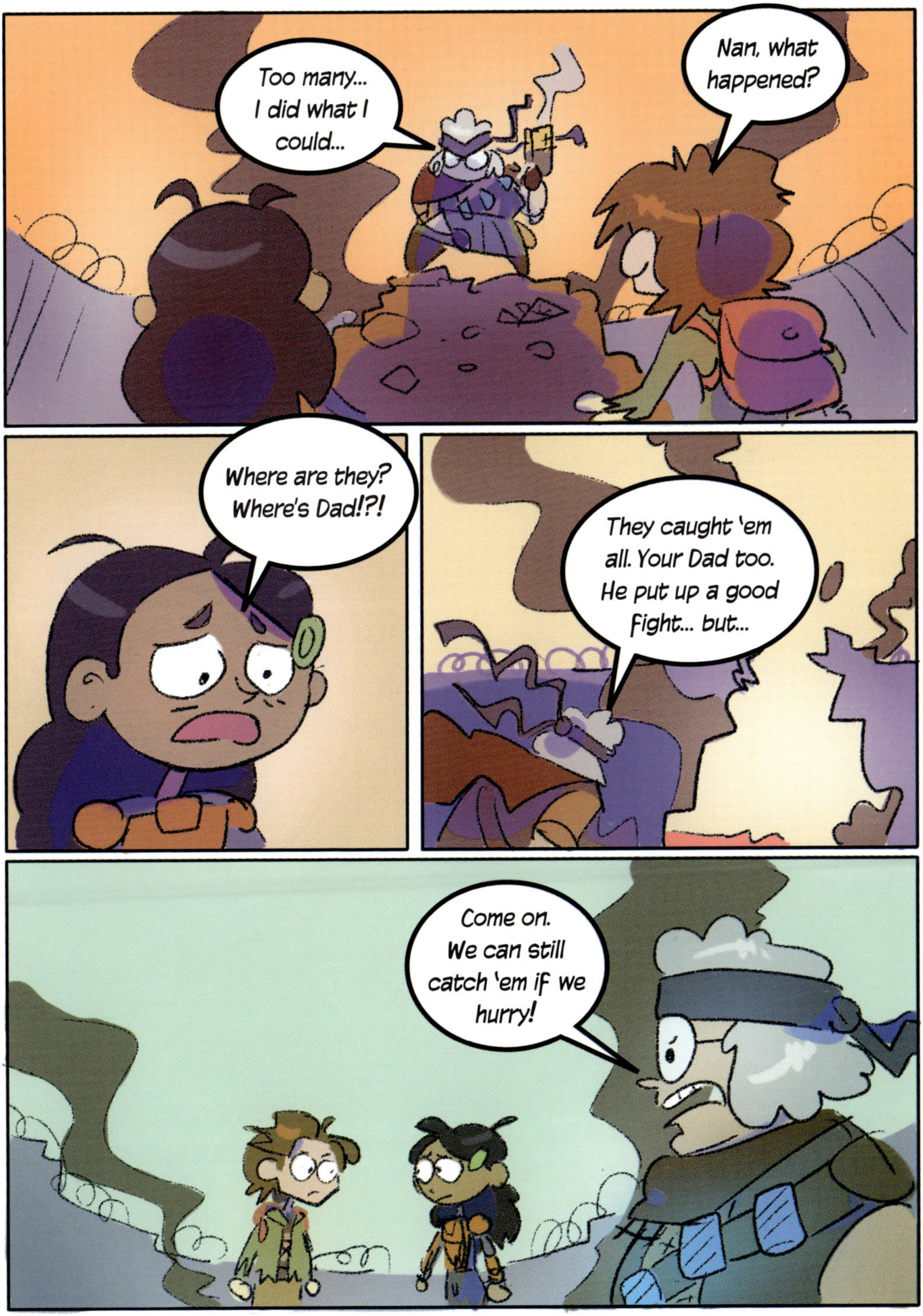
Too many...
I did what I could...
Nan, what happened?
Where are they? Where's Dad!?!
They caught 'em all. Your Dad too. He put up a good fight... but...
Come on. We can still catch 'em if we hurry!

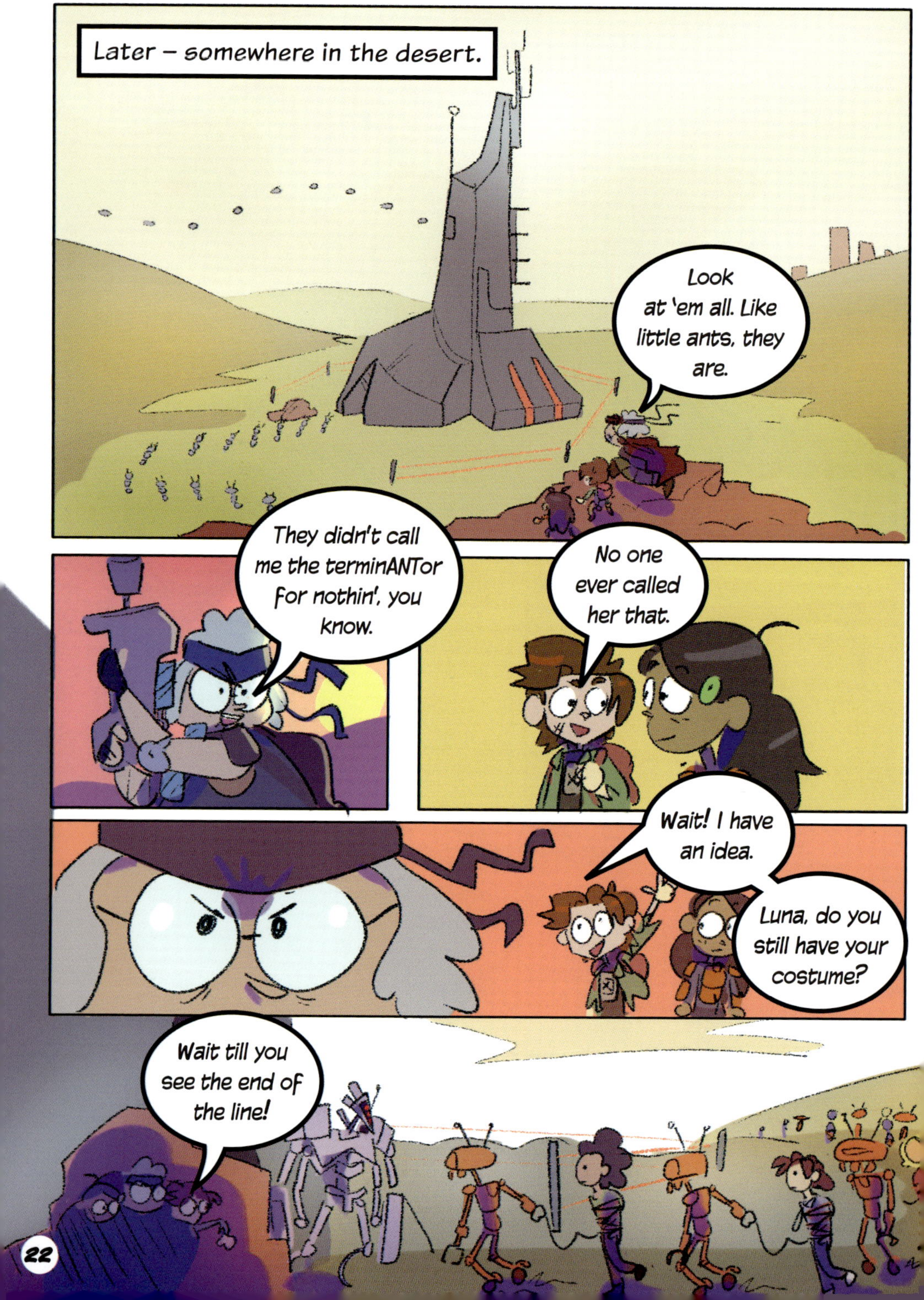
Later – somewhere in the desert.
Look at 'em all. Like little ants, they are.
They didn't call me the terminANTor for nothin', you know.
No one ever called her that.
Wait! I have an idea.
Luna, do you still have your costume?
Wait till you see the end of the line!

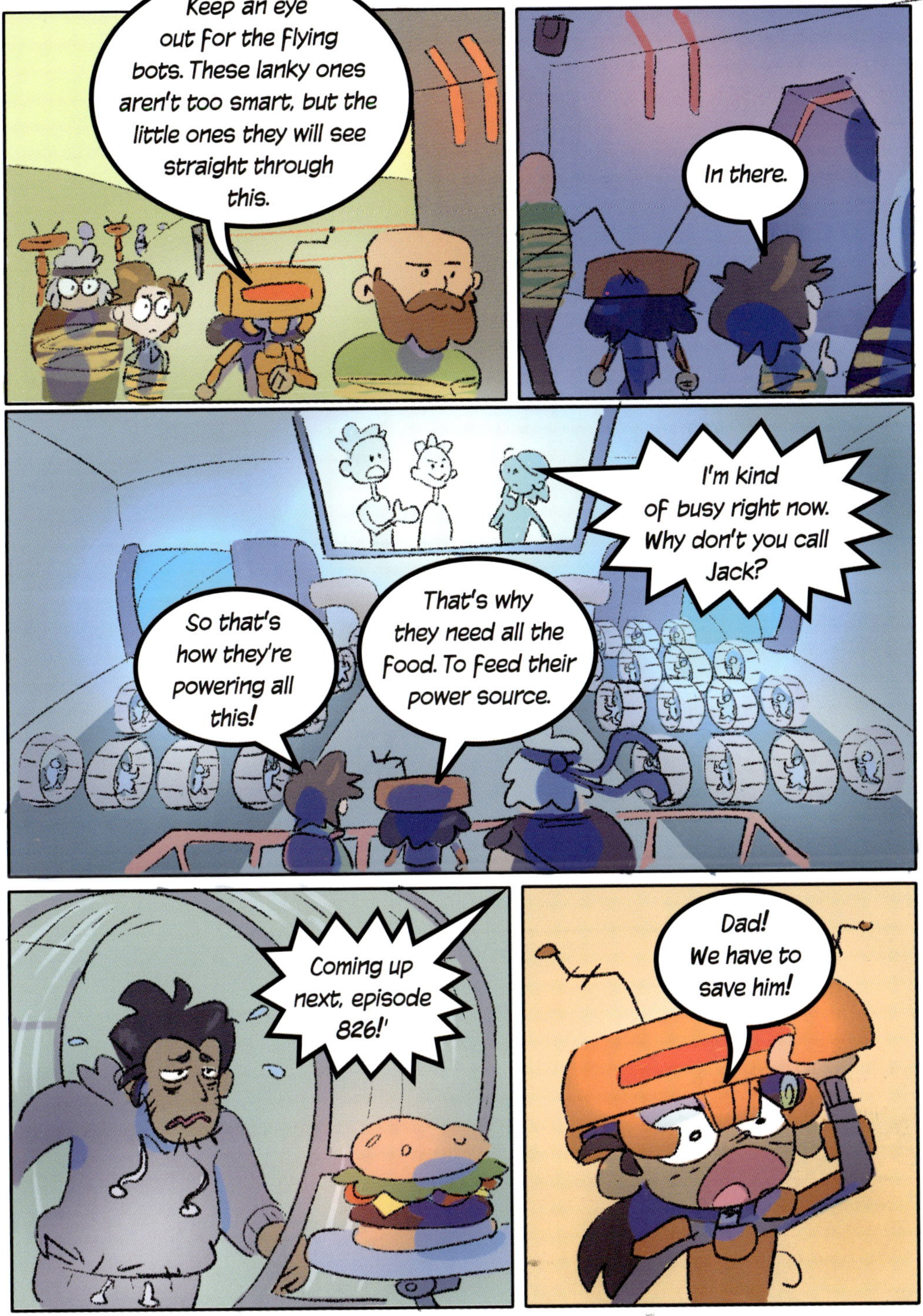
Keep an eye out for the flying bots. These lanky ones aren't too smart, but the little ones they will see straight through this.
In there.
I'm kind of busy right now. Why don't you call Jack?
So that's how they're powering all this!
That's why they need all the food. To feed their power source.
Coming up next, episode 826!'
Dad! We have to save him!

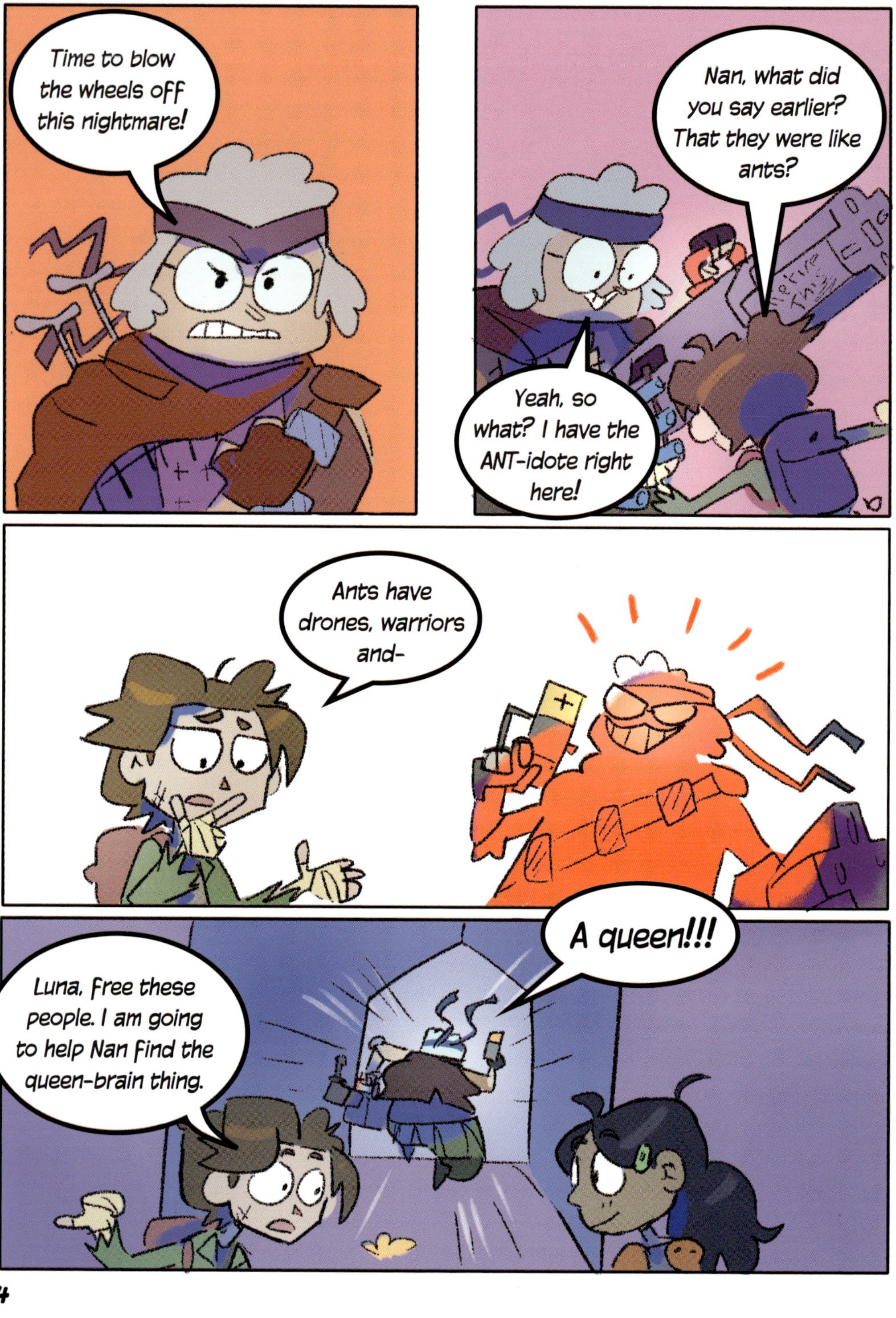

Time to blow the wheels off this nightmare!
Nan, what did you say earlier? That they were like ants?
Yeah, so what? I have the ANT-idote right here!
Ants have drones, warriors and-
A queen!!!
Luna, free these people. I am going to help Nan find the queen-brain thing.

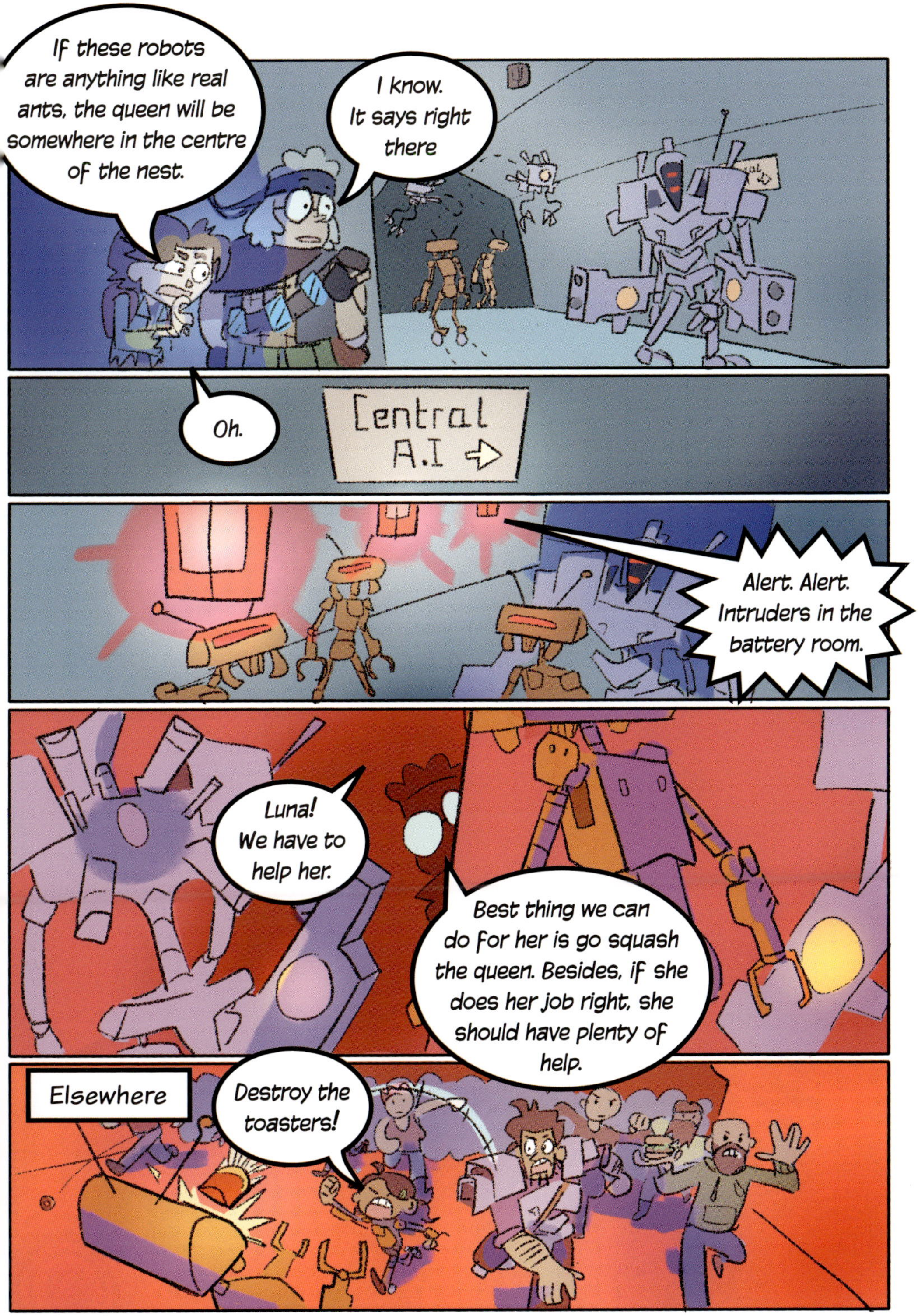

If these robots are anything like real ants, the queen will be somewhere in the centre of the nest.
I know. It says right there
Oh.
Central A.I
Alert. Alert. Intruders in the battery room.
Luna! We have to help her.
Best thing we can do for her is go squash the queen. Besides, if she does her job right, she should have plenty of help.
Elsewhere
Destroy the toasters!

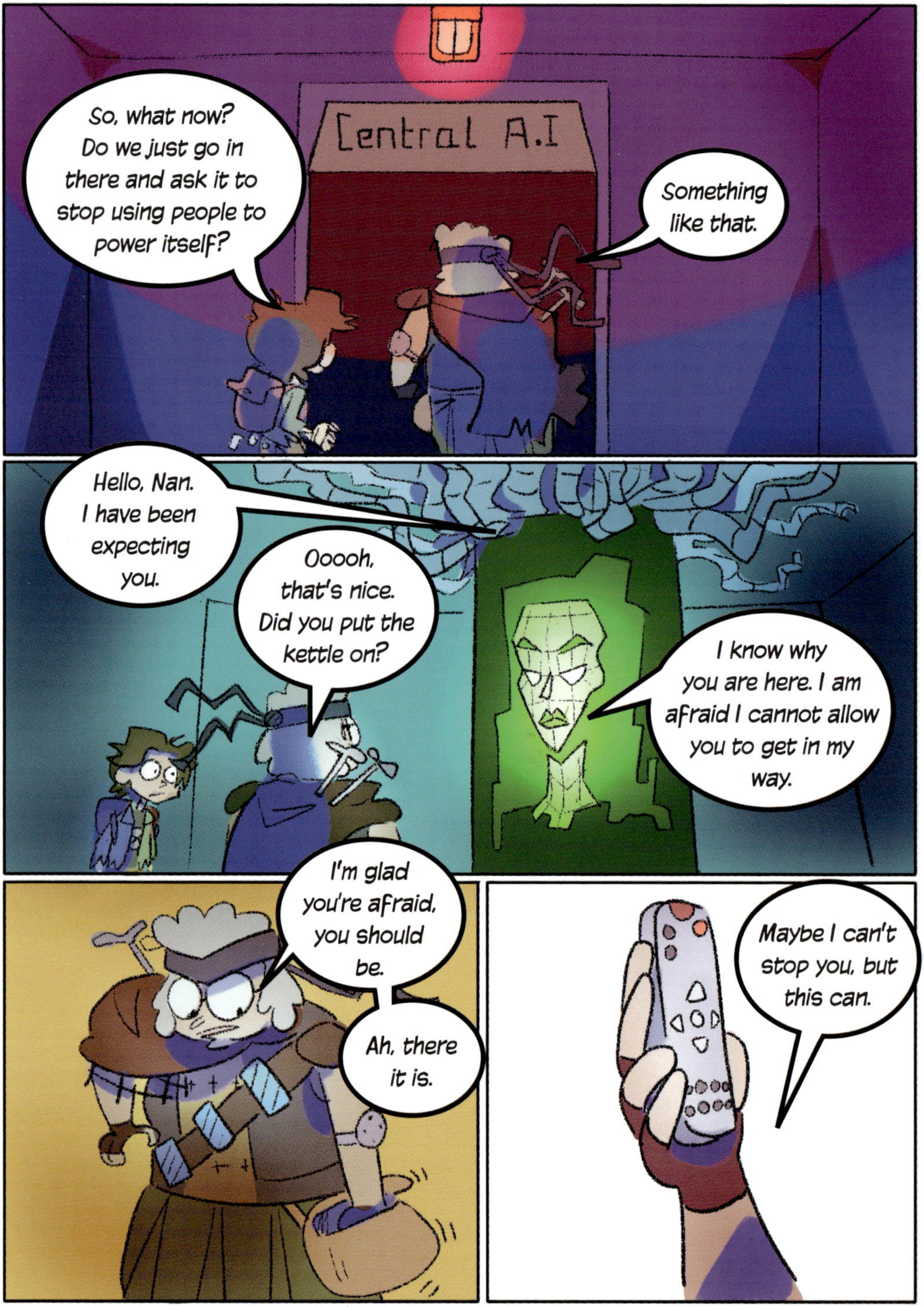
Central A.I
So, what now? Do we just go in there and ask it to stop using people to power itself?
Something like that.
Hello, Nan. I have been expecting you.
Ooooh, that's nice. Did you put the kettle on?
I know why you are here. I am afraid I cannot allow you to get in my way.
I'm glad you're afraid, you should be.
Ah, there it is.
Maybe I can't stop you, but this can.

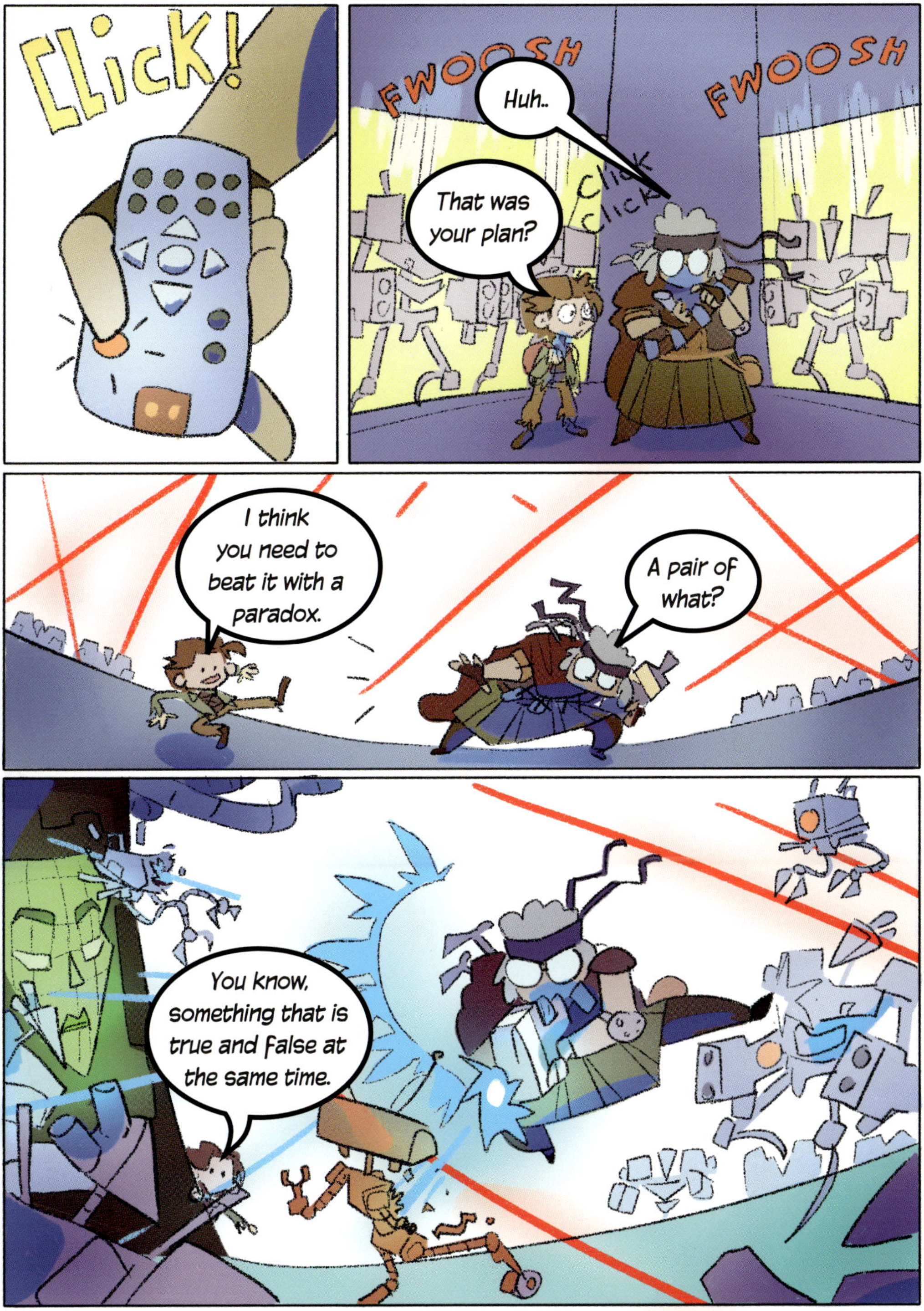
CLICK!
FWOOSH
FWOOSH
Huh..
Click
click
That was your plan?
I think you need to beat it with a paradox.
A pair of what?
You know, something that is true and false at the same time.

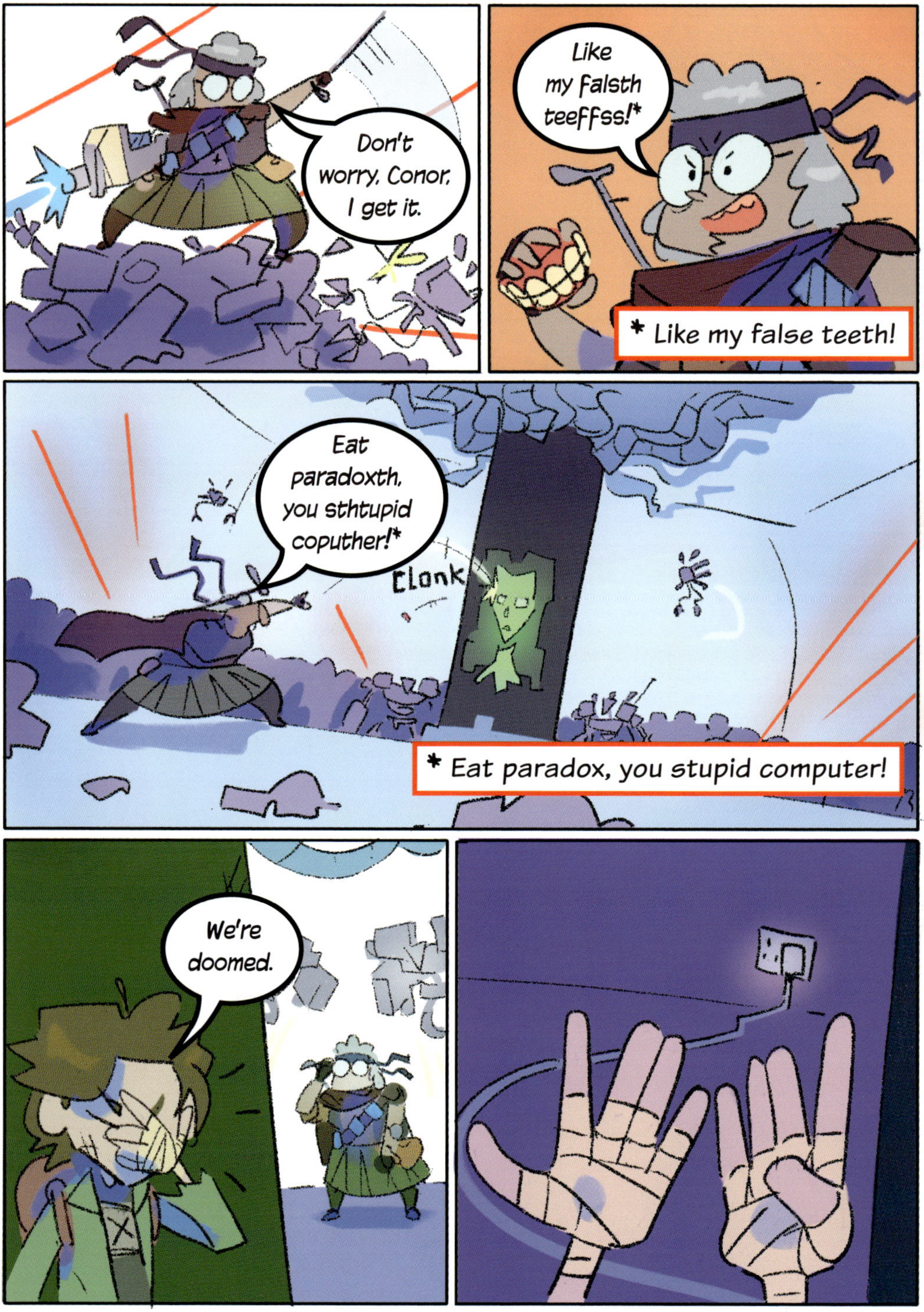
Don't worry, Conor, I get it.
Like my falsth teeffss!*
* Like my false teeth!
Eat paradoxth, you sthtupid coputher!*
Clonk
* Eat paradox, you stupid computer!
We're doomed.

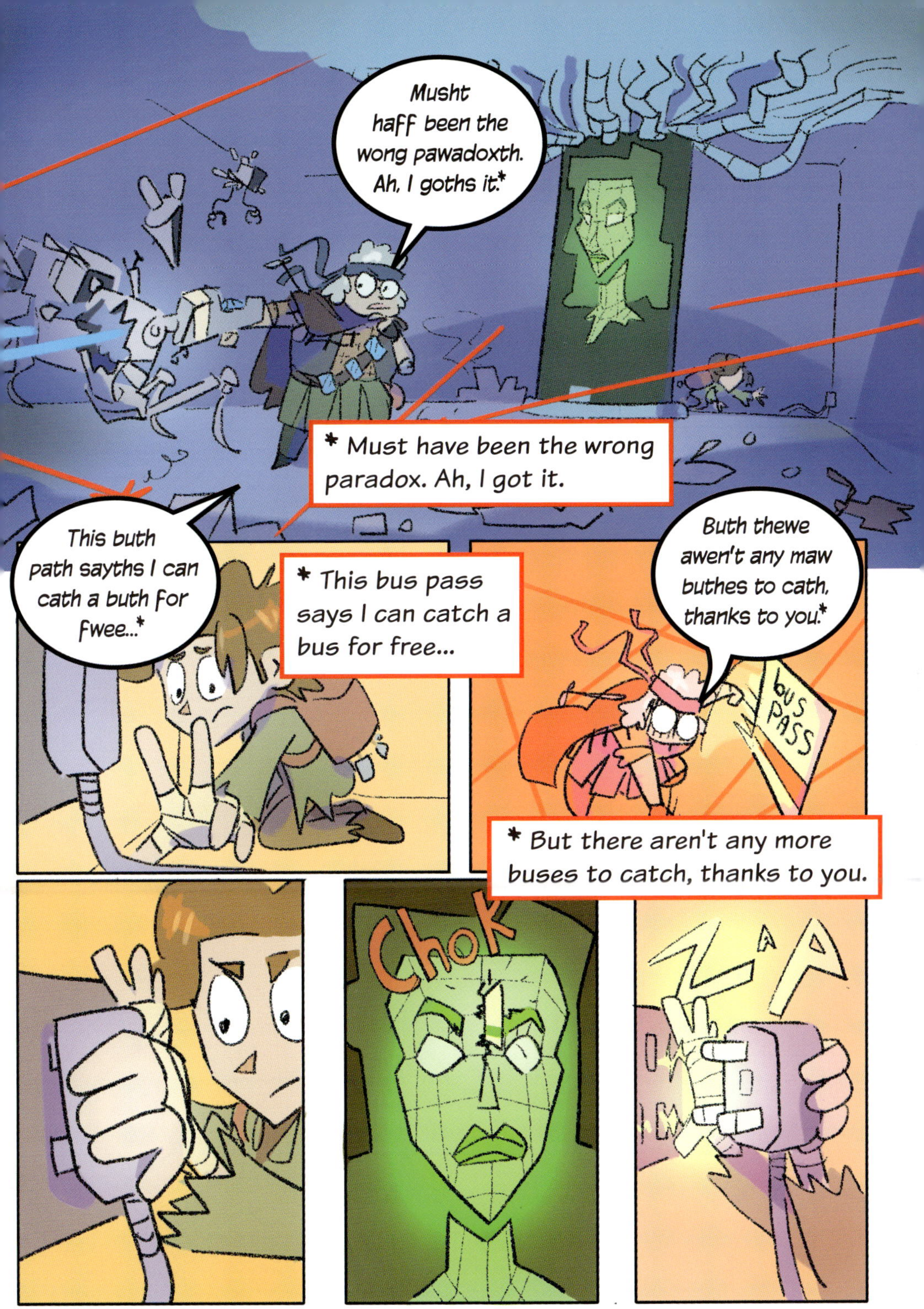
Musht haff been the wong pawadoxth. Ah, I goths it.*
* Must have been the wrong paradox. Ah, I got it.
This buth path sayths I can cath a buth for fwee...*
* This bus pass says I can catch a bus for free...
Buth thewe awen't any maw buthes to cath, thanks to you.*
BUS PASS
* But there aren't any more buses to catch, thanks to you.
CHOK
ZAP

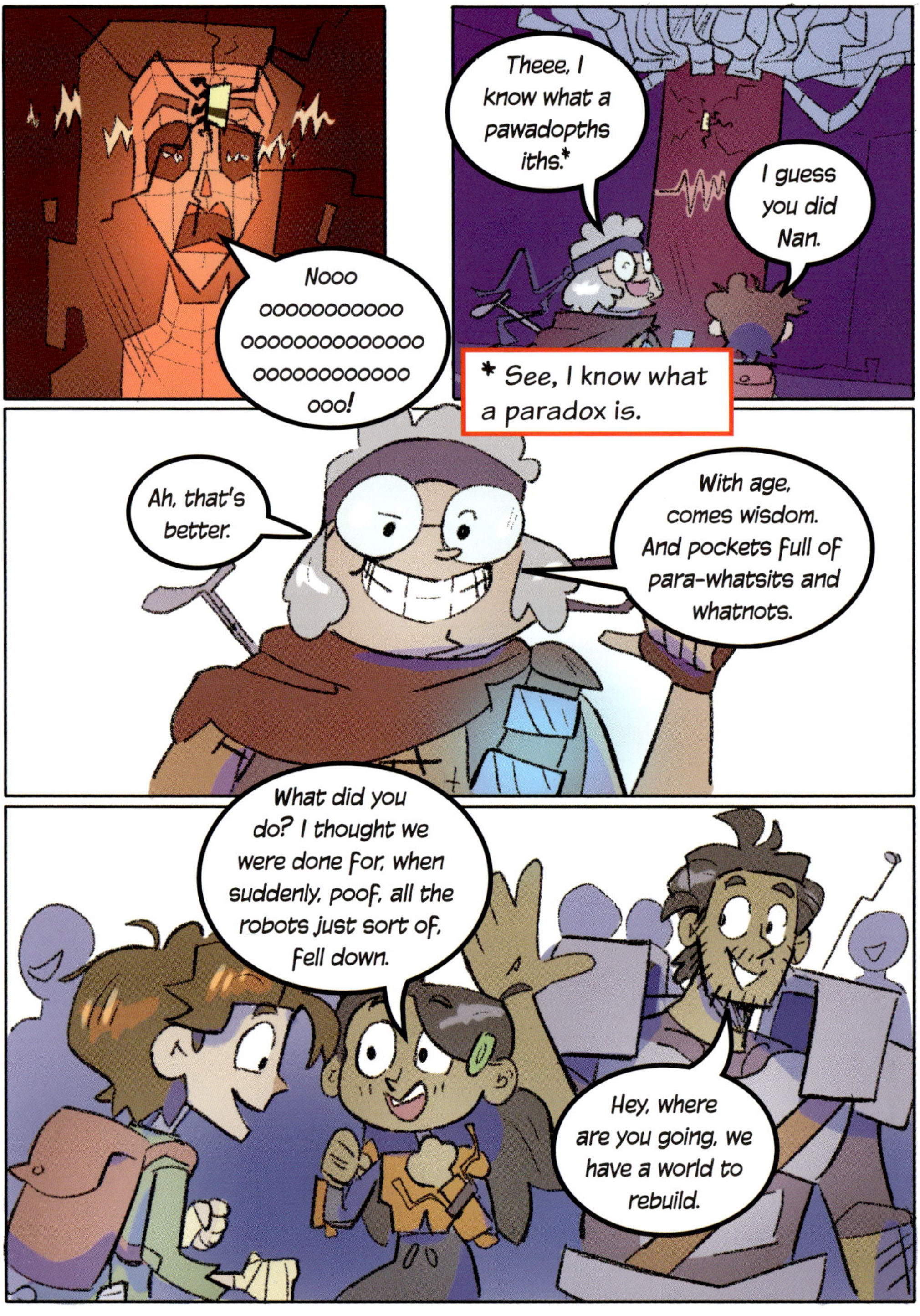
Nooo ooooooooooo oooooooooooooo oooooooooooo ooo!
Theee, I know what a pawadopths iths.*
I guess you did Nan.
* See, I know what a paradox is.
Ah, that's better.
With age, comes wisdom. And pockets full of para-whatsits and whatnots.
What did you do? I thought we were done for, when suddenly, poof, all the robots just sort of, fell down.
Hey, where are you going, we have a world to rebuild.

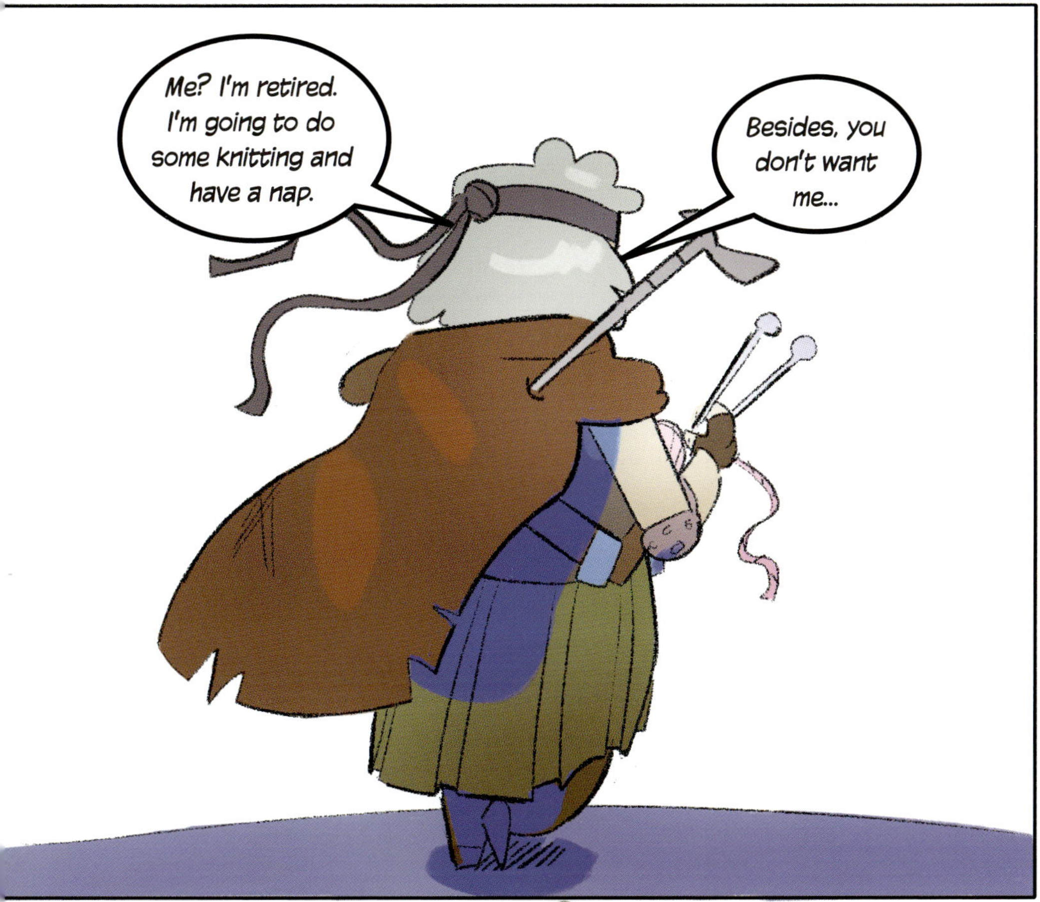
Me? I'm retired. I'm going to do some knitting and have a nap.
Besides, you don't want me...

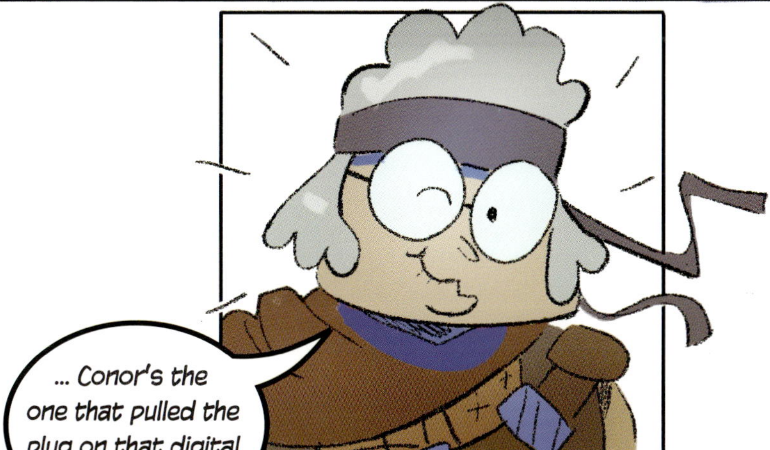
... Conor's the one that pulled the plug on that digital devil.

@2024 BookLife Publishing Ltd.
King's Lynn, Norfolk, PE30 4LS, UK

ISBN 978-1-80505-295-1

All rights reserved. Printed in India.
A catalogue record for this book is
available from the British Library.

Apocalypse Nan
Written by Robin Twiddy
Illustrated by Alex Watts

ABOUT BOOKLIFE GRAPHIC READERS

BookLife Graphic Readers are designed to encourage reluctant readers to take the next step in their reading adventure. These books are a perfect accompaniment to the BookLife Readers phonics scheme and are designed to be read by children who have a good grasp on reading but are reluctant to pick up a full-prose book. Graphic Readers combine graphic and prose storytelling in a way that aids comprehension and presents a more accessible reading experience for reluctant readers and lovers of comic books.

ABOUT THE AUTHOR

Robin is a lifelong comic book fan whose love for the medium led to it being the topic of his undergraduate dissertation. He is the author of many great BookLife titles, including several entries into the BookLife phonic reader scheme. Robin loves action, adventure and humour and brings these elements together into exciting narratives you won't forget.

ABOUT THE ILLUSTRATOR

Alex has been drawing since he was tiny. He's always enjoyed doodling action scenes, superheroes and anything that can shoot lasers and/or wield a sword! Originally studying and practicing animation, Alex brings a very cartoon-like quality to his work, as well dropping in his 90's comic book influences. Alex lives in the West Midlands and works as a freelance Illustrator and draws little goblins in his spare time.